D0221033

THE BUDGET PUZZLE

The Budget Puzzle

UNDERSTANDING FEDERAL SPENDING

John F. Cogan, Timothy J. Muris, and Allen Schick

Stanford University Press, Stanford, California
1994

Stanford University Press
Stanford, California

Printed in the United States of America

CIP data appear at the end of the book

Stanford University Press publications are distributed exclusively by Stanford University Press within the United States, Canada, and Mexico; they are distributed exclusively by Cambridge University Press throughout the rest of the world.

Preface

IN early 1989 the authors began a series of discussions about the problem of the federal budget and how research has contributed to understanding its dynamic. Each of us had devoted several years to understanding the forces that have shaped the budget. One of us had spent most of his professional career researching and writing about the federal budget process. The others had served as policy officials at the Office of Management and Budget. What brought us together was a shared recognition that the rapidly rising national debt is one of the most serious financial problems facing the country and the belief that much of the problem stems not just from the politics of the budget, but from the institutional structure within which budget decisions are made.

We believe that, although research over the years has contributed much to understanding the powerful dynamics that drive the budget, the complexity of the budget and the congressional process requires a new approach to advance the frontiers of knowledge regarding the budget. The approach emphasizes micro rather than macro budgeting. It studies the budget as a system of interrelated but separate decisions that determine spending levels on individual programs and groups of programs. It focuses on the committee system, the rules and procedures Congress uses, the way in which budget outcomes are measured and reported to the public, and how the factors interact to produce budget outcomes. This book is the first product of our effort toward research on microbudgeting. It was written before President Clinton took office and therefore contains no reference to the Clinton administration. The Clinton administration's first year is now complete, and we believe that its results do not alter in any way the strength or force of the conclusions we reach in the individual chapters.

We gratefully acknowledge the financial support of the Smith Richardson Foundation through grants to the Hoover Institution.

Contents

Figures and Tables

FIGURES

TABLES

THE BUDGET PUZZLE

1

Why Study Microbudgeting?

ALLEN SCHICK

SHORTLY before the 1990 congressional elections, presidential aides and congressional leaders put the finishing touches on deficit-reducing legislation that many of them hoped would be the budget deal of the century. Despite protracted disagreement over some of the details, both executive and legislative negotiators wanted a package that would be sufficiently large to put the deficit problem behind them. To accomplish this, they cobbled together a politically balanced package of revenue enhancements, spending cuts, and new budget enforcement rules that was projected to pare approximately $500 billion from the federal budget deficit over a five-year period. In enacting the Omnibus Budget Reconciliation Act of 1990 (OBRA), the long-warring branches looked ahead to a period of budget tranquility and rapidly declining deficits.

It didn't take long, however, for optimism about the budget to dissipate. Within weeks after OBRA was signed into law, revised budget estimates issued by the Congressional Budget Office revealed further deterioration in the government's fiscal condition. The estimated deficit for fiscal 1991 (the first year covered by the deal) had ballooned more than $50 billion above previous projections, and comparable overruns were foreseen for subsequent years. The bad news was confirmed by the fiscal 1992 budget, which produced a record $290 billion deficit. Three years after OBRA was enacted, the prospect of achieving a satisfactory budget condition seemed as remote as it had been before, impelling newly elected President Clinton to propose, and Congress to enact, another $500 billion deficit reduction package.

What went wrong? The simple, widely accepted explanation is that a torrent of "uncontrollable" bad news had pushed the deficit higher. Military operations in the Persian Gulf had added greatly to expenditures while a spreading recession had subtracted significantly from revenues. The deepening crisis in savings and loans and banking had boosted claims on the budget, as had the continuing rise in health care costs. The comforting message was that the escalating deficit was not the work of budget-busting politicians but of forces largely beyond their control. Moreover, the bulging deficit was welcomed by many experts as a much-needed stimulus to the faltering economy. Although the deficit was much higher than had been previously forecast, politicians took comfort in the conviction that it was much lower than it would have been had OBRA not been passed.

These no fault explanations had a familiar ring. They had been used before to excuse failures in U.S. budget policy, and given the persistence of high deficits, they will be used again. But rather than merely rationalizing budget failure, these explanations tend to make matters worse. They do so by distorting public perceptions about the deficit and by assuring politicians that there is little more they can or should do to remedy the problem.

By presenting the budget predominantly in terms of the totals, such as the $500 billion reportedly trimmed from the 1991–95 deficit, politicians lose sight of or choose to ignore the manner in which the savings have been computed and the assumptions that underlie them. They permit themselves to be blissfully ignorant of what has been swept under the budgetary rug, and they ask few questions about how the totals have been computed or why past deficit-reduction efforts have fallen so far short of the mark. Their macrobudgetary perspective gives short shrift to key determinants of budget outcomes, such as the behavior of politicians and the incentives and opportunities they have to conceal or misstate the true impacts of their actions. The net results have been rosier budget forecasts than are warranted, and budget outcomes that are much less favorable than the public has been led to expect.

The totals are only the tip of the budgetary iceberg. Below the surface is the busy, confusing world of cross-pressured politicians striving to reduce the deficit while protecting or expanding popular programs. The budgetary cross-pressures are deeply rooted in

American public opinion, but their damaging impact on budgetary behavior has been aggravated by two contemporary conditions: huge deficits and divided government. Alarm over seemingly intractable deficits has impelled politicians to act in ways that make it appear that they are doing something about the problem; divided government (protracted Republican control of the White House and a Democratic majority in one or both houses of Congress) until the 1992 election greatly hampered negotiations to reduce the deficit. One way out of this budgetary conundrum has been to make exaggerated claims of success in curtailing the deficit. Under the guise of reducing the deficit, cross-pressured politicians typically cut spending less than they claim to, and they sometimes add to it.

In the end, of course, a budget's totals are the sum of its parts. Most of the deficit-reduction drives mounted in the 1980–90 period failed because the claimed cuts added up to less than the targeted totals. To fully comprehend this policy failure, we must adopt a microbudgetary perspective: the budget must be broken down into its basic elements; the assumptions pertaining to each program or account must be carefully reviewed, and the methods by which savings are computed must be critically examined. These are not easy tasks. Since the 1960s, research on federal budgeting has been oriented to macro issues, such as the interaction between key budget aggregates and economic conditions. Few studies have been conducted on the formulation of budgets by federal agencies or on the manner in which the appropriations subcommittees mark up their bills.

The shift from macro- to microbudgeting represents more than a reorientation from the totals to the parts. In political terms, it reflects a clash between the preference of Americans for smaller government and their demands for bigger programs. One consequence of this contradiction in public opinion is that the budget's totals often appear to be less than the sum of its parts. To understand this arithmetic feat, one must investigate the manner in which budget programs and accounts are decided, labeled, and "scored." As a research problem, this entails a shift from synoptic issues such as growth rates and fiscal impacts to more focused concerns such as the behavior of appropriations committee members in satisfying their constituents' expectations while upholding their self-proclaimed role as guardians of the treasury. When one turns to these questions, it becomes apparent that the methods appropriate for the study of microbudgeting are not the same as those applied to macrobudgeting. Nor are the findings likely to be the same, for the federal budget's totals are never quite the sum of its parts.

When one decomposes the budget into its salient parts, previously obscured or neglected facets are revealed. These offer important lessons for both budget policy and the organization of the budget process.

Perhaps it is asking too much to hope that a decade from now neither politicians nor other policymakers will take the budget's totals at face value without first asking how the numbers have been derived. Only when the budget's totals are understood in terms of the parts on which they are built will it be possible to control the deficit effectively.

To be sure, in budgeting the totals always are important. Total revenue and spending, the balance between them, and the rates at which they change are among the principal means by which governments define their budget policies and objectives, and also are convenient indicators used by the media and interested citizens to appraise government performance. The totals are a simple but politically important report card of how well the government is doing in handling public funds and in meeting public expectations. Perennial concerns, such as the size and fiscal condition of the government, are monitored by looking at the totals. At all levels of government, gapsmanship—closing or narrowing the projected gap between total revenues and expenditures—dominates the budget preparation process.

The Age of Macrobudgeting

For macrobudgeting to flourish, it is essential not only that the totals matter—they almost always do—but that the totals result from government decisions, not from conditions beyond its control. The federal budget was primed for a macro role by the economic boom following World War II and by the acceptance of Keynesian doctrine as the dominant influence on U.S. fiscal policy. Sustained economic growth made the budget's totals appear to be the willed outcomes of effective policy making. For budget makers, the welcomed Keynesian message was that the skillful regulation of aggregate demand would keep the economy on the path of stable growth and promote both low inflation and high employment. The heady success of this formula in the early 1960s gave the government confidence that command of the totals would enable it to achieve valued objectives, such as a strong economy and well-financed public programs, by adapting the budget process to these ends.

The conduct of an active fiscal policy required that the government permit the totals to vary from their original targets. Yet efficacious budgeting demanded that the variances be the result not of policy drift or feebleness but of purposeful guidance of the economy. Two tools of dynamic fiscal policy—fine-tuning and built-in stabilizers—drove home the idea that while the totals might be in a state of flux, the end result would be the right one. Fine-tuning meant that by making many small adjustments in the budget, the government would avoid having to make big, jarring ones. Built-in stabilizers meant (as the term suggests) that even though adjustments were automatic, they were congruent with the government's budget policy, not antagonistic to it. The government would have the best of budget worlds: totals that changed but were still controlled by it.

For a time, macrobudgetary policy delivered what it promised. The best years were the period from the ascension of John F. Kennedy in 1961 to the Vietnam-driven overheating of the U.S. economy approximately five years later. This was not a long period, but it left a legacy of budgetary practices and ideas that persisted even when the economy faltered and the Keynesian intellectual hegemony was challenged. The influence of macro policy was evident in the prominence accorded economic guidance as one of the basic functions of presidential budgeting. But this influence also pervaded the core processes of legislative budgeting. In devising its own budget process in 1974, Congress sought to model its operations after the presidential process. Congress coveted the President's capacity to decide the totals and expected its own spending control to be greatly enhanced if it could do the same. Accordingly, the 1974 Budget Act provided for Congress to adopt annual budget resolutions that would set forth total revenues and outlays, the projected deficit, and the public debt for the following fiscal year.

Prior to the Budget Act, Congress did not vote on total outlays or the deficit; these were just the arithmetic results of the many separate decisions taken each year. Yet Congress has not greeted this added chore with enthusiasm. In some years, it has been hard to marshal support for a budget resolution; in others, the budget totals have been underestimated to ease the task of adopting a budget resolution. As the 1990s opened, Congress's budget process was superseded by sequestration procedures, caps on discretionary spending, and summit negotiations between presidential aides and congressional leaders. The budget resolution process remains in operation, but it is not the principal means by which Congress decides budget totals and priorities.

Shortcomings of Macrobudgeting

There is reason to expect macrobudgeting to find a more hospitable environment in the executive branch than in Congress. But even in the executive branch, there are limits on what macrobudgeting can accomplish. The macro budget is dependent on micro behavior. The experiences of the 1960s, the heyday of macrobudgeting, reveal two shortcomings that continue to plague budgetary practice to this day. One is that the totals cannot be effectively controlled unless the parts are tracked and managed; the other is that preoccupation with the totals encourages legerdemain that conceals their true size.

In futile efforts to control the budget, Congress enacted a series of spending limitations in the late 1960s and early 1970s. As I showed in *Congress and Money*, none of the five approaches tried between 1967 and 1973 worked.[1] In that pre–Gramm-Rudman-Hollings period, Congress did not resort to automatic procedures. Yet, the dismal results of that era bear an eerie resemblance to the abortive deficit controls enacted in the 1980s. The failure of spending controls in the 1960s spurred enactment of a new congressional budget process in the 1970s. The failure of the "discretionary" budget controls of the 1974 act spurred the enactment of automatic sequestration in the 1980s. And the failure of deficit controls in the 1980s led to the imposition of spending controls in the early 1990s. Congress has come full circle in less than twenty-five years, but whether it has gained more skill in dealing with the budget is open to question.

In fact, controlling total expenditures is a much more difficult task today than it was a quarter century ago because much more of the budget is allocated to mandatory expenditures such as entitlements and interest charges. According to published OMB data, between 1965 and 1990 mandatory payments (many of which are open-ended) doubled as a percentage of total federal outlays, from 30 to 60 percent.[2] Decisions on the totals cannot be enforced when so much of the budget is linked to exogenous factors. The 1990 Budget Enforcement Act abandoned control of the deficit (which is the net total of all budget transactions) and shifted instead to caps on discretionary expenditures (that is, spending controlled by annual appropriations) and to "pay as you go" rules, which require that legislated increases in entitlements be offset by cuts in other entitlements or by revenue increases.[3] Yet under the new rules, budget totals, including the deficit, are allowed to float upward as impelled by inflation and other economic conditions, war-related and other emergency expenditures, certain re-estimates, and various preferential categories. In effect, the 1990 act legitimizes the totals as the sum of the budget's parts.[4]

Whether the revised rules are more effective than the ones they replaced—they are certainly less ambitious—is likely to depend on whether the government comes to grips with another shortcoming of macrobudgeting: the totals are often distorted by the inclination of politicians to portray the budget in an unrealistically favorable light. The incentive to mislead flourishes even in good times, as Kamlet and Mowery found in their detailed study of budget preparation during the Eisenhower, Kennedy, Johnson, and Nixon presidencies.[5]

The temptation to play fast and loose with the numbers grows as the condition of the budget deteriorates and as budget controls, especially those pertaining to the totals, are made more stringent. These conditions played havoc with budget controls in the late 1960s, as the cost of the Vietnam War and the size of the deficit escalated. Understating the cost of the war was only one of the deceptions practiced during that troubled period. Another was to shift assisted housing from up-front financing to an accounting scheme that spread the cost over twenty years or more. This device enabled the government to report much smaller outlays for housing without actually reducing expenditures. Other schemes involved the sale of "participation certificates" and other "pooled" loan assets, which enabled the government to understate the cost of its lending operations.[6] When the Federal Financing Bank was established in 1973, fresh opportunities became available for removing transactions from the budget.[7]

The government has tried from time to time to eliminate gimmicks by adopting new accounting rules or by restoring items to the budget. This was one of the objectives of the 1967 report of the President's Commission on Budget Concepts, which designed the unified budget.[8] Other initiatives were taken in the 1974 Budget Act, the Gramm-Rudman-Hollings Act, and the Budget Enforcement Act. The repeated drives to curb budgetary gimmickry attest to the futility of these efforts in the face of powerful political incentives to mislead.

The assumptions on which budget calculations are based have also gained prominence as budget policy has become increasingly tied to baseline computations. In Chapter 5, I will discuss Timothy Muris's revealing study on this subject. For the present, it bears noting that whenever savings or deficit reductions are claimed, they are computed in terms of (usually unpublished) baseline assumptions. Projected savings are achieved, therefore, only to the extent that the assumptions are valid. The most convenient way for politicians to paint a brighter future for the budget or to claim that they are coming to grips with the deficit is to manipulate the assumptions. Inasmuch as it is virtually impossible to devise tamperproof assumptions that are free of political influence, the budget's totals will continue to be hostage to optimistic assumptions about its parts.

The Breakdown of Macrobudgeting

Just as the perceived success of macroeconomic fiscal policy prompted parallel developments in budgeting, declining confidence in Keynesian prescriptions has spurred a rethinking of budgetary concepts. The influence of Keynesian ideas was closely related to the vigor of the economy. When economic performance faltered in the 1970s, confidence in the capacity of the government to manage aggregate demand sagged. In a period of stagflation—high inflation and low growth—it was hard to devise a budget strategy to alleviate one of these ills without worsening the other. With the government unable to steer a stable fiscal course, the supportive interaction of the budget and the economy deteriorated, and fiscal policy became prey to frequent lurches.[9] As the decade wore on and the sense of fiscal enfeeblement deepened, Richard Nixon's 1971 boast, "Now I am a Keynesian," was supplanted by a babble of conflicting ideas vying for legitimacy and attention.

The two most prominent of the new schools of thought, rational expectations and supply-side economics, differed on important matters but both disdained macroeconomic solutions to fiscal problems. Proponents of rational expectations rejected countercyclical responses on the grounds that they are likely to be ineffective. Because intervention is expected—the budget is always adjusted to spur a weak economy—the impact is discounted before it is felt. Supply-side economics sought to shift policy attention from total demand to the behavior of individual producers and investors. Supply-siders saw the economy as the cumulative impact of the countless actions and decisions by all participants in economic activity. What is important, they argued, is the effect of government policies on individual incentives to work, produce, save, and invest. For supply-siders, the economy as a whole has no policy significance except as the sum of individual behaviors. Some advocates of supply-side economics regard the size of the deficit as inconsequential, but the more pronounced influence of this school of thought has been on microeconomic policy. Although supply-side tenets have been derided by many mainstream economists, they have spurred such sweeping policy changes as the 1986 tax reform, which reduced the highest marginal tax rate on individual income from 50 to 33 percent.[10]

Just as the weak economy called established fiscal policy into question in the 1970s, seemingly intractable deficits paralyzed macrobudgetary policy during much of the 1980s. With deficits persistently much higher than politicians professed to want, and much higher than budgeted levels as well, it was not tenable to insist that they were the result of willful policy decisions. Rather, big deficits denoted policy impotence, as did some of the political responses to them such as the automatic sequestration rules. One lesson from almost two decades of budgetary frustration is that the deficit cannot be controlled by dictating what the totals should be. It can be controlled only by paying attention to individual revenue and spending decisions.

Institutional Breakdown

The intellectual disrepair of macrobudgeting has been paralleled by a serious deterioration in institutional capacity. Historically, macrobudgeting has been the domain of the White House, microbudgeting the *terra cognita* of Congress. It was the inability of a fragmented Congress to integrate budgetary policy that led it to cede budgetary power to the President in the Budget and Accounting Act of 1921. In the seventy years since the establishment of the presidential budget process, the annual budget submitted to Congress has contained detailed requests for federal programs and accounts, as well as projections of total outlays and the deficit. These totals have generally set the boundaries within which Congress has acted on the budget's many parts. If it were to exceed the President's totals, Congress would be open to the charge that it was busting the budget; if it stayed within the totals, Congress would be seen as fiscally responsible yet would still have considerable discretion to rearrange the parts. Over the years, this cooperative relationship enabled the President to get his way on macrobudgetary issues and Congress to write its priorities into particular programs.

To say that the President was the dominant player in shaping the totals is not to deny his interest and influence with respect to the particulars. Each President had an agenda, and each had to be vigilant that Congress would not undercut his budgetary leadership by greatly rearranging priorities or by introducing new gimmicks that made it possible to stretch the totals. But each President generally bowed, sometimes after a tussle, to the reality that the legislative branch would put its own stamp on the budget.

How did a fragmented Congress manage to stay within (or close to) the President's totals while acting on each of the parts? The answer is critical to understanding the interaction of micro- and macrobudgeting and to the relationship between the two branches. Congress adhered to the totals by using the President's budget as a reference point for its decisions on individual programs and accounts. Every step of the way, the appropriations committees compared their actions to the President's estimates. In so doing, they could be confident that incremental adjustments in various accounts would add up to acceptable totals.

The budgetary division of labor protected each branch's salient interests. The President could keep the budget within bounds, integrate it into economic policy making, and have the lead role in defining the scope of government. Congress could respond to local pressures and prevail on many of its particular budgetary preferences. This convenient arrangement depended on the President asking for large enough totals to accommodate Congress on the parts. Most Presidents implicitly cooperated with Congress's budgetary interests by asking for a sufficiently large increase each year to enable Congress to spend more on its favored programs while "cutting" the budget.

In the 1970s and 1980s, a series of related factors destabilized this comfortable arrangement. (1) The growth and indexation of open-ended entitlement programs made total spending and the deficit more sensitive to exogenous conditions and less responsive to presidential policies. (2) Congress introduced baseline computations, which are independent of the President's budget recommendations, as the main reference point for many of its actions. (3) The persistence of huge deficits discouraged recent Presidents from submitting realistic budgets. (4) Congress meddled in macrobudgeting by adopting budget resolutions that set forth its own budget totals. (5) President Reagan frequently intervened in congressional microbudgeting by demanding significant reductions in domestic expenditures.

The last two of these developments indicate a far-reaching breakdown in the budgetary relationship between President and Congress. By taking a more independent role in macrobudgeting, Congress seriously weakened the President's capacity to control the totals. When the President took a more aggressive role in microbudgeting, he degraded the usefulness of his budget as a reference point for congressional action. Corresponding to the changes in the President's role was a reorientation of the Office of Management and Budget (OMB) from an agency that managed the executive budget process to one that devotes much of its resources to monitoring congressional budget actions.[11] This adjustment was under way before the 1980s, but it was given additional impetus by David Stockman's personal involvement in the legislative process and his determination to make OMB more alert to congressional developments.[12] But as the White House became more attuned to congressional actions, the President's budgetary performance deteriorated. Although it was a necessary adjustment to reality, the reorientation to Congress attenuated OMB's traditional role. In the past, its budget work was tied to the President's recommendations; now, it has to recalculate the numbers whenever Congress takes one of its many budget-impacting actions. Where the President once led, Congress now has substantial initiative. Thus, OMB has found it necessary to develop a formal SAP (Statement of Administration Policy) process for notifying Congress of White House objections to pending appropriations bills.[13]

To function as the chief macrobudgeter, the President must produce totals that are sufficiently realistic that Congress will use them to guide its own budget work. Some Reagan and Bush budgets have failed this test. While the "dead on arrival" label pinned on some of their budgets by the media may have been an overstatement, recent budgets have been opening gambits, not real statements of presidential intentions. Realism has been driven out by gargantuan deficits and by the transformation of the President's budget from an authoritative statement of policy into the opening bid in a negotiations process with congressional leaders. In the 1980s, the White House came to see the budget as a legislative proposal that would, like other measures, be rewritten by Congress. The President understood that because the real budget emerges only in give-and-take bargaining between the two branches, it would be foolhardy for him to show his true preferences at the start of the process.

The Budget Committees: Congress's Macrobudgeters

Within Congress, macrobudgeting has been entrusted since 1975 to the House and Senate budget committees. But these committees have a severely circumscribed role in microbudgeting, which has greatly weakened their capacity to speak for Congress on the budget's totals. Under the legislative division of labor established by the 1974 Budget Act, the budget committees have a role in setting the budget aggregates and in allocating funds to approximately twenty broad functional categories such as health, income security, and national defense. However, these committees are *not* permitted to line-item their budget resolutions by specifying the programs to be funded. The budget committees often refer to specific programs in reports accompanying the budget resolution or reconciliation instructions, but these assumptions are not binding on the affected committees. In fact, other committees—particularly the appropriations committees—often ignore the functional allocations set forth in budget resolutions and section 302/602 reports.[14]

There have been periods during the fifteen-year history of the congressional budget process when the budget committees exercised considerable influence on outcomes by having their microbudgetary assumptions used as the basis for legislative action. These periods generally occurred when other participants (such as the President or the appropriations committees) saw the budget resolution as an opportunity to advance their own budgetary interests. In recent years, however, the budget committees have had few allies, and their influence has waned to the point where it hardly matters whether the budget resolution is adopted at all.

Walled off from substantive microbudgetary influence, the budget committees have learned that jurisdiction over the totals can be a thankless chore. The primary job of the budget committees is to get members of Congress to vote on such unpleasant matters as the deficit or total outlays, votes they would not have to make if there were no budget process. Worse yet, many members see these as substantively meaningless, though politically important, votes. Lacking effective control of the parts, the budget committees cannot always defend the totals when they are pushed higher by congressional actions or other factors, nor can they attract support for their policies by earmarking funds to particular programs or constituencies.

The concentration on totals partly explains why the budget committees usually have a hard time getting their resolutions through Congress. In contrast to appropriations bills, which have constituencies and are often approved by lopsided majorities, budget resolutions typically squeak through with razor-thin margins.[15] Moreover, budget resolutions normally are adopted on party-line votes, while appropriations bills usually are supported by majorities of both parties. The parties tend to be polarized by macro issues such as the appropriate overall size of the budget or of the deficit, as well as by "intermediate" issues such as functional priorities. But in voting on appropriations bills, members of Congress are inclined to set aside partisan differences so they can get on with the rewarding business of dividing the pie among favored programs or projects.

The macrobudgetary role of the budget committees is inherently flawed. These committees have extraordinarily broad scope but little power. Though composing only a small fraction of total House or Senate membership, these committees reach to the interests of virtually every other congressional committee. Congress has neutralized the extraordinary scope of the budget committees by denying them any legislative jurisdiction.[16] (Note the parallel with the Joint Economic Committee, Congress's other "macro" committee, which also lacks legislative jurisdiction.) In their early years, the budget committees compensated for their legislative weakness by playing on the strong determination of congressmen to make the new process work. But as the novelty of the process wore off, the budget committees were compelled to accommodate the interests of others in order to get their resolutions adopted. In the 1980s, they became increasingly dependent on party leaders both to shape policy and to round up the votes. By the end of the decade, the budget resolution merely recorded or ratified decisions made elsewhere, principally in summit negotiations; they no longer were the means by which Congress actually resolved budget issues.

The evolution of congressional budgeting suggests that party leaders may be the only viable legislative spokesmen for the totals. They alone can speak for Congress at budget negotiations with the White House, and they are best situated to obtain legislative endorsement of interbranch agreements. Nevertheless, leadership intervention in budget issues is likely to occur only spasmodically, not as an ongoing responsibility. Recent leadership activism may be a by-product of divided government and of the protracted impasse between the two branches over the budget. In these circumstances, the White House might welcome strong negotiating partners in Congress who can commit the votes needed to get implementing legislation reported by committees and passed by the House and Senate. If, however, one party were to control both branches, the President might prefer to work with compliant congressional leaders too weak to stake out an independent position on the budget. Over time, party leaders are also likely to be hemmed in by congressional committees, which value their independence and do not want to be beholden to bargains struck by others. The difficulties experienced by Democratic leaders in getting legislative approval of the 1990 deficit-reduction package indicates that they cannot always deliver on their budget promises.[17]

In macrobudgetary dealings with the President, Congress tends to be the weaker partner. The White House can manipulate the totals by relying on optimistic economic assumptions. In fact, the more unrealistic the assumptions, the greater the advantage the executive branch has vis-à-vis Congress. After striving to stake out an independent position on the economy in the early years of the budget process, Congress gave up the effort in the 1980s and accepted the President's economic assumptions as the basis for its budget resolutions. Congress had little choice in the matter, for sticking to its own economic forecasts would have yielded much higher deficits than had been projected by the White House.

In pushing for a macrobudgeting role, Congress's main impact has been to challenge the President's leadership, not to strengthen its own capability. When it comes to budget totals, just about everybody feels weaker than they once did. Macrobudgetary power has been dissipated; nobody has much of it anymore.

2

The Dispersion of Spending Authority and Federal Budget Deficits

JOHN F. COGAN

SINCE the 1950s, deficit spending has been a persistent characteristic of federal government finance. In only five years since 1950 has the federal government's budget been balanced. Worse, the federal government's balance sheet has significantly deteriorated in each decade. The steadily increasing budget deficits have brought the national debt to nearly $40,000 per American household.

The persistent budget deficits are an extraordinary phenomenon in American history. Throughout most of the nation's history until World War II, a balanced federal budget was the norm. The federal government did incur budget deficits during years of economic contractions and in times of armed conflict but would return to balancing the budget in years following these events. The continual failure in the post–World War II era to balance nonrecessionary, peacetime budgets is without precedent.

The existence of the persistent postwar deficits has thus far defied unified explanation. In the popular press each decade's deficits have their own unique explanation. In the 1960s, it was the simultaneous effort to fight the war on poverty and the Vietnam War. In the 1970s, it was economic stagnation. In the 1980s, it was major tax cuts and a large defense buildup. Although each of these explanations is in some sense correct, there appears to be a more systematic and fundamental force at work.

This chapter examines the role that the Congressional budget process has played in contributing to the emergence of the persistent post–World War II federal budget deficits.[1] My central thesis is that two key institutional changes made by the Congress during the 1930s were critically important in producing the nearly continuous string of postwar deficits. The first and most important change was to transform the jurisdiction over expenditures from a highly centralized congressional committee structure in each house to a widely decentralized committee structure. The modern process of spreading spending jurisdiction among committees began in 1932 when the Reconstruction Finance Corporation was created and financed outside the normal appropriations procedure. The decentralization process accelerated during the next four decades. By the mid-1970s, almost every substantive congressional committee in each house of Congress had authority to report legislation to the floor committing funds from the U.S. Treasury.

Broadening spending authority created what is known as a common resource problem.[2] The common resource is general-fund revenue. The problem is that when many congressional committees have authority to spend general-fund revenue, no individual committee has any incentive to restrain its spending commitments since the total level of spending is beyond any single committee's responsibility. The result is an accelerating rate of expenditures relative to general revenues until the available revenue pool is exhausted and deficit financing is relied upon.

A second institutional change, also occurring in the Congress at about the same time, exacerbated the consequences of the proliferation of spending committees. This change was the creation of tax-financed trust funds—for example, Social Security, Medicare hospital insurance. Establishing tax-financed trust funds and placing jurisdiction over them primarily in the tax-writing committees created incentives for the tax-writing committees to substitute trust-fund revenues for general-fund revenues.

The combination of these two institutional changes drove general-fund expenditures upward and general-fund revenues downward relative to Gross National Product (GNP). The result was ever-increasing general-fund and total budget deficits.

The outline of this chapter is as follows: The first section provides a summary of trust fund and general fund expenditures, and revenues during the postwar period. Next I discuss the institutional changes in committee jurisdiction that have occurred since the 1930s and the reasons why these changes would be expected to produce the observed tax and spending outcomes in the two budgets. I then examine three prior periods in American fiscal history in an effort to test the committee-proliferation hypothesis: 1789 to the late 1870s, when almost all spending was under the jurisdiction of one committee in each House; the early 1880s to 1920, when spending jurisdiction was splintered among a half-dozen committees; and 1921–30, when appropriations jurisdiction was once again consolidated in a single committee in each house. Evidence is found of a sizable increase in expenditures and the incidence of deficits from the early 1880s to 1920. An equally dramatic halt in the growth of expenditures and a return to balanced budgets is found in the 1920s. The next section examines the budget behavior of the tax-financed trust fund and the trade-off between trust-fund and general-fund revenues. The final section summarizes the evidence and draws conclusions.

Postwar Budget Trends

Figure 2.1 illustrates the growing mismatch between federal revenues and expenditures that has been characteristic of the federal budget thoughout the post–World War II era.[3] Since the Korean conflict, federal expenditures have risen relative to Gross Domestic Product (GDP) from 18 percent in 1955 to 23.5 percent in 1990. Federal revenues relative to GDP, on the other hand, are remarkably constant. Revenues exhibit only a slight upward drift during the postwar period. Since the mid-1950s, taxes as a percentage of GDP have ranged outside the 17.5–19.5 percent interval only three times.

Trends in total budget revenues and expenditures mask dramatically divergent trends that have taken place between the trust-fund and general-fund components of the budget. Before describing these distinct trends, it is important to understand the essential differences between trust-fund and general-fund programs.

Most expenditures on trust-fund programs are financed by a specific tax levied on the public.[4] The proceeds from trust fund taxes flow into a special account in the budget, and program expenditures are made by withdrawing funds from the account. Trust

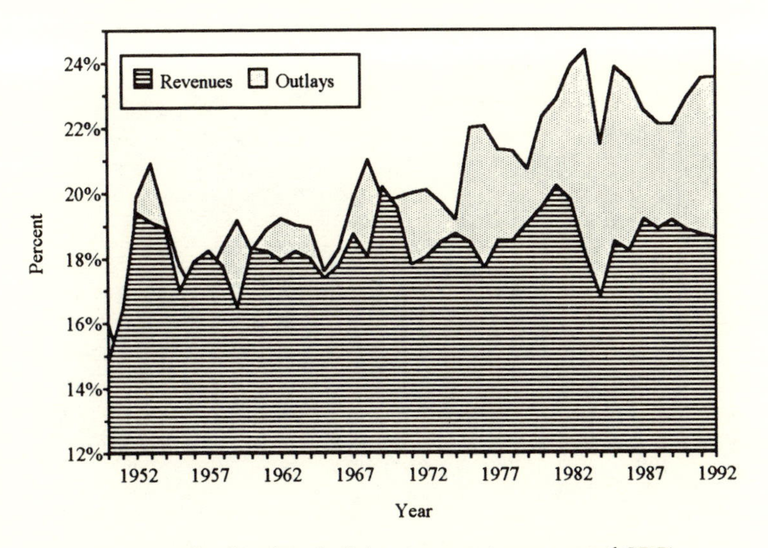

FIGURE 2.1. Federal Budget Deficit, 1950–92 (as percent of GDP)

fund tax revenues can be used only to support the activities of the trust fund program and therefore are "dedicated revenues."

General fund programs, on the other hand, are not financed by any specific revenue source. Instead, revenues from a multitude of sources are pooled together in a common fund used to finance a broad array of general fund activities ranging from national defense to grants to study the migratory patterns of certain birds.

Figures 2.2 and 2.3 depict revenues and expenditures separately for trust fund and general fund programs during the period 1950–92. As Figure 2.2 illustrates, trust fund revenues and expenditures have been in approximate balance throughout the postwar period. Neither large surpluses nor large deficits persist for any significant time. Surpluses, such as those that emerged in the early 1950s and those during the late 1960s and early 1970s, have been quickly eradicated by expansions in spending or economic contractions. Deficits, such as those which occurred in the late 1950s, mid-1970s, and early 1980s, have been quickly eliminated by a combination of increases in dedicated taxes and reductions in benefits.

In contrast, as illustrated in Figure 2.3, an enormous gap has opened up between expenditures and revenues in the general fund.

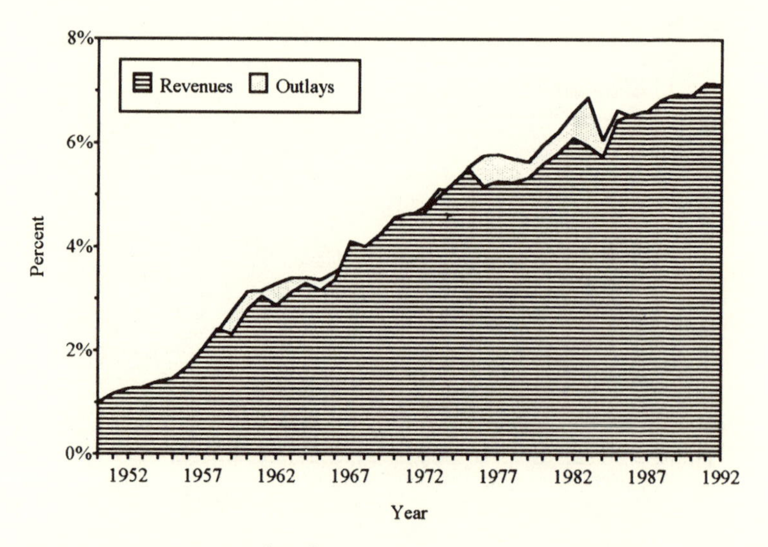

FIGURE 2.2. Trust Fund Deficit, 1950–92 (as percent of GDP)

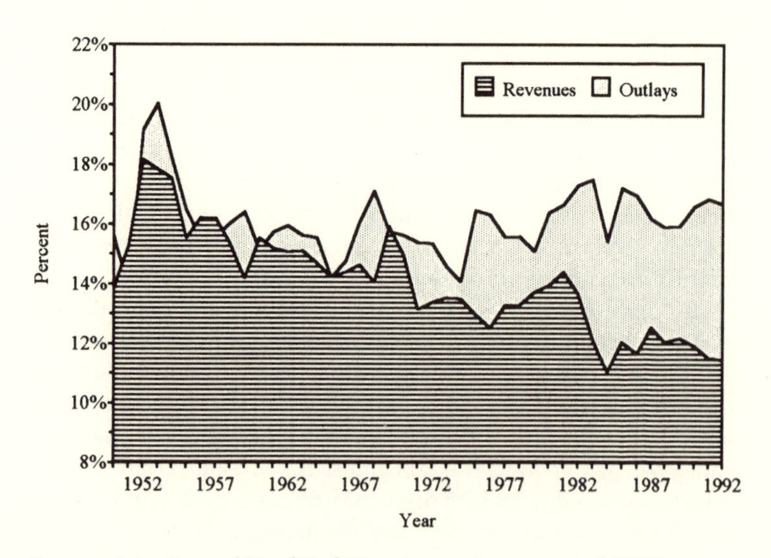

FIGURE 2.3. General Fund Deficit, 1950–92 (as percent of GDP)

TABLE 2.1
Total Budget and General-Fund Deficits, 1950–92
(percent of GDP)

Period	Total budget	General fund
1950–59	0.4%	0.8%
1960–69	0.8	0.9
1970–79	2.1	2.2
1980–89	4.3	4.3
1990–92	4.6	5.6

SOURCE: Executive Office of the President, OMB, *Budget and Budget Appendix of the U.S. Government*, FY 1952–92.

Both the time path and the magnitude of the general fund deficit match the time trend and the size of the total budget deficit. In fact, in an accounting sense, the entire postwar growth in the total budget deficit is attributable to the general fund deficit. Table 2.1 provides a quantitative dimension to this relationship; both the total and general-fund deficits have risen in lockstep; from less than 1 percent of GNP in the 1950s to around 4.5 percent of GNP during the 1980s.

As the trends in Figure 2.3 and the data in Table 2.1 suggest, the forces producing the persistent budget deficits have been operating on the general fund for the entire postwar period and possibly longer. Although the budget deficits of the 1980s and 1990s are much larger than those of prior decades, they represent a continuation of previous trends.

Figures 2.2 and 2.3 also reveal the existence of an apparent systematic substitution of trust-fund revenue for general-fund revenues during the postwar period. While total budget revenues have been remarkably constant at around 18–19 percent of GDP, trust revenues have risen steadily and general taxes have declined significantly. Since the mid-1950s, trust revenues have risen from just under 2 percent to almost 8 percent of GNP by the early 1990s. In contrast, general revenues have declined from almost 16 percent of GNP during the mid-1950s to just slightly over 11 percent of GNP in the mid-1980s.[5] The almost dollar-for-dollar substitution of trust for general revenue relative to GNP suggests that increases in trust-fund taxes may be crowding out general-fund taxes.

The coexistence of chronic general-fund deficits and balanced trust-fund budgets is a paradox. Why does the Congress adhere to the principle of a balanced budget in the trust funds while opening up a massive fiscal imbalance in the general fund? Clearly, the forces that have been at work in producing the former have been absent from the latter. A natural place to begin an analysis of these forces is the difference between the institutional mechanisms the Congress employs in making its fiscal decisions in each of the two budgets.

The Dispersal of Spending Power: 1932–1974

In the general fund, the Congress currently exercises its power of the purse through a highly decentralized committee system. In each house no single congressional committee has responsibility for all general-fund financial decisions. Instead, jurisdiction over expenditures is divided among a multitude of committees. How the jurisdiction over expenditures is divided in a given Congress depends as much on tradition, politics, and the powers of particular committees as it does on the formal rules of each house of Congress.

In the modern Congress, various financial mechanisms have been employed to facilitate the operation of dispersed spending power. Some techniques, such as permanent appropriations and borrowing authority, completely bypass the annual appropriations process. Others, such as appropriated entitlements and contract authority, technically require annual appropriations, but by the time the appropriation decision is made, the budget resources have already been effectively committed. Thus, for programs financed through the latter techniques, the appropriation is regarded as a pro forma decision.

Table 2.2 displays the current (1992) distribution of general-fund program outlays among congressional committees.[6] In each house, the Appropriations Committee has jurisdiction for over two-thirds of all general outlays. Jurisdiction for programs covering the remaining 30 percent of general outlays is spread among seventeen House and thirteen Senate legislative committees. The large share accounted for by the Ways and Means Committee reflects its jurisdiction over several major entitlements, including the Aid to Families with Dependent Children program, Supplemental Security Income, and its shared jurisdiction over Medicare

TABLE 2.2
Distribution of General-Fund Expenditures by House Committee, 1992 and 1932

	Percent of General Fund Outlays
1992	
Appropriations	63%
Energy and Commerce	11
Ways and Means	7
Agriculture	6
All Other	13
1932	
Appropriations	89%
Post Office	7
All Other Committees	4

SOURCE: *Budget, 1934; 1984*. See Appendix A for details. For comparability, the distribution of total budget outlays for 1982 is provided in Appendix A.

physician and outpatient services with the Energy and Commerce Committee. The Energy and Commerce Committee's 11 percent share primarily reflects the importance of appropriated entitlements for health care—for example, Medicaid and its portion of Medicare.

The wide distribution of spending authority among congressional committees is a relatively recent phenomenon. Table 2.2 compares the current distribution to the distribution that prevailed in 1932. The year 1932 is chosen as a point of reference because it immediately predates the first of a series of legislative actions that dispersed spending authority. In that fiscal year, borrowing authority was not in use. And contract authority had been granted only in a few isolated instances. The only major entitlement was veterans' benefits. Although there were numerous permanent appropriations, their combined outlays were small. As the data in Table 2.2 show, the Appropriations Committee maintained control over the lion's share of spending.[7] The only other committee that had any significant authority over spending was the Post Office and Post Roads Committee. In each house, no other committee controlled more than 1.5 percent of the total.

The broadening of spending authority during this fifty-year period did not result from identifiable changes in key congressional rules or changes in the organization of committees. Instead, it occurred as a result of a series of separate legislative actions creating spending mechanisms that effectively committed budget resources either independently or in advance of formal appropriations.

If any single legislative activity marks the beginning of the modern process of broadening spending authority, it was the creation of the Reconstruction Finance Corporation (RFC) in 1932. In creating the RFC, the appropriations process was circumvented by permitting the RFC to borrow directly from the U.S. Treasury. Never before had such a funding technique been used.[8] But soon it would be used to finance numerous agencies and programs. Within the next five years, the Commodity Credit Corporation, Tennessee Valley Authority, Homeowners Loan Corporation, Rural Electrification Administration, and Federal Public Housing Authority were created and allowed to obtain financing through the same mechanism.

By the early 1950s, seventeen programs located in nine executive branch agencies had been given borrowing authority.[9] By the late 1950s, borrowing authority had been extended to more than thirty programs, including farm and housing subsidies, civil defense activities, college housing loans, area redevelopment projects, and the Export-Import Bank.[10] In the early 1970s, the use of borrowing authority by the legislative committees peaked. However, by this time the effects of another legislative device—appropriated entitlements—were driving the general-fund budget.[11]

The appropriated entitlement has become the most important mechanism that Congress has employed to spread general-fund spending authority among its committees. Table 2.3, indicating the importance of entitlements, provides a list of the major general-fund entitlements, each program's date of enactment, and the funding level for each program. Together, these fifteen entitlements account for 88 percent of all general spending under the jurisdiction of committees other than Appropriations. Although appropriated entitlements have existed since the beginning of the nation, most major entitlements were created during two relatively recent periods: the 1930s and 1965–74.

Prior to the 1930s, major entitlements were limited to payments to individuals who had performed some specified service in govern-

TABLE 2.3
Major Entitlement Programs

	FY 92 Outlays ($ in millions)
Veterans Compensation (1789)	$17,296
Military Retirement (1861)	24,491
Civil Service Retirement (1920)	34,001
Commodity Credit Corporation (1933)	16,635
Aid to Families with Dependent Children (1935)	15,104
Old Age Assistance (1935)	
Aid to the Blind (1935)	19,445[a]
Aid to the Permanently and Totally Disabled (1950)	
Food Stamps (1964)	21,804
Medicaid (1965)	67,827
Medicare (Part B) (1965)	50,285
Guaranteed Student Loans (1965)[b]	4,803
Social Services Block Grant (1965)	2,708
Earned Income Tax Credit (1975)	7,345
Child nutrition programs (1972)	6,146
Subtotal	$287,890

SOURCE: *Budget*, 1984.
NOTE: Excludes major entitlements that are primarily financed with dedicated tax revenues. Year in parenthesis is date the program was enacted or placed on an entitlement basis.
[a]These programs were combined to form the Supplemental Security Income program in 1972.
[b]Obligations are used instead of outlays, which are not available.

ment: disabled veterans and retired military and civilian government personnel.[12] During the economic emergency of the 1930s, general-fund entitlements were expanded to include persons who had not performed any direct government service, such as farmers, and state governments to assist in providing aid to poor single mothers, the aged, and the blind. Nearly thirty years later, another group of major general-fund entitlements was established. This group provides health and nutrition entitlements directly to individuals and financial assistance entitlements to states and local governments, educational agencies, and banks for various services.

Throughout the forty-year period of increasingly decentralized budget decision making, the Congress made several attempts at consolidating spending authority. The most important of these was the 1974 Budget Control and Impoundment Act.[13] The 1974 act restricted some forms of spending that were used by the legislating committees, in particular, borrowing authority and contract authority. It also restricted somewhat the ability of Congress to create *new* entitlement programs but left those then in existence untouched. Moreover, the Congress was unwilling to impose any significant new decision-making apparatus on the existing decentralized structure. It simply superimposed what amounted to a coordinating committee, the Budget Committee, on top of the existing fragmented decision-making process. In doing so, it failed to address the fundamental incentives for additional spending and against retrenchment that a fragmented system provides.[14]

Why both houses of Congress beginning in the 1930s chose to broaden spending authority among its committees and why it was done in such a piecemeal fashion over the forty-year interval are unanswered questions. Undoubtedly the forces that produced the majority sentiment in favor of broadening spending authority were similar to those operating to increase expenditures. In this sense, the broadening of spending authority was in part a mechanism by which the Congress chose to achieve a desired objective. However, once in place, the decentralization of spending authority would be expected to have a causal impact on the growth in spending and deficit financing.

The process by which this occurs works as follows: In making budget decisions with respect to programs under its jurisdiction, each congressional committee attempts to be responsive to the wishes of those concerned about the adequacy of program benefits. But each committee also recognizes that any increased benefits must be financed. Thus, each committee faces a trade-off. On the positive side, increases in program benefits produce certain "rewards" to committee members from those who are recipients of the higher benefits. On the negative side, the greater benefits must somehow be paid for, either by higher current taxes or deficit financing.

However, the size of the overall tax burden or the deficit is beyond the control of any single committee. The political blame for the tax or deficit consequences of higher spending is shared by all committees. Thus, each committee reaps the full political rewards of higher expenditures on its programs, but each committee bears only a portion of the adverse political consequences of financing higher expenditures. Faced with this situation, each committee rationally concludes that it should spend more on its programs. This conclusion, of course, is reached by all committees. The result is that the combined spending by all committees exceeds what it would have been had each committee borne the full consequences of its actions.

In a dynamic setting, this process feeds upon itself. With each round of the budget process, every committee has the opportunity to observe the spending behavior of all other committees. The other committees, in response to the incentives provided by the multiple committee system, are observed to spend an ever-increasing amount on programs within their individual jurisdictions. Repeated observations of these actions serve to reinforce the individual committee's belief in the futility of practicing fiscal restraint and the wisdom of raising expenditures on programs within its jurisdiction. Competition among the separate committees soon develops.

The competition is fueled by the actions of the special interests. Special-interest groups begin to exert pressure on the individual committees to ensure that each group retains its "fair share" of the total budget. No individual committee has any institutional reason for resisting these pressures. With divided spending jurisdiction, each committee's institutional role is confined to the programs under its jurisdiction. Each committee, observing the behavior of the other committees, knows that it can maintain its fair share of the total only by increasing spending on its programs by at least as much as other committees. Each committee becomes locked in by the competitive forces that compel it continually to raise the level of spending on its programs.

The problem created by widely distributed spending authority is analogous to similar problems that arise whenever there are many competing claimants for a common resource. To illustrate, imagine a publicly owned forest that is opened to any and all logging companies who desire access to it. No individual company would have any reason to restrain its logging activities. In fact, each company would have every incentive to cut down as many trees as it could before a competitor did so. In this setting, the inexorable forces of competition would inevitably lead to the depletion of the forest. The depletion would not necessarily occur, however, if only one logging company was given access to the forest. A single logging company that had sole ownership rights to the forest would not only preserve some of the trees for later use but would also act to replenish the depleted supply of trees that resulted from its current harvesting operations.[15]

There are more than theoretical reasons for believing that the wide distribution of spending authority would have severe fiscal consequences. In earlier periods, many members of Congress argued that a wide distribution of spending authority would inevitably lead to increased spending and budget deficits. Perhaps the most forceful of such arguments was made over a century ago by one of the House of Representatives' most distinguished members, Samuel Randall. During his career, Mr. Randall had been both Speaker of the House and chairman of the Appropriations Committee. In 1885, in response to a proposal to divide the jurisdiction over appropriations among several congressional committees, Mr. Randall offered the following warning: "If you undertake to divide all these appropriations and have many committees where there ought to be but one you will enter upon a path of extravagance you cannot foresee the length of or the depth of until we find the Treasury of the country bankrupt."[16]

Chairman Randall was not alone in his view. The *Congressional Record* and other historical documents contain numerous similar statements by other national leaders, ranging from James Garfield to Woodrow Wilson.[17]

But more importantly, there is considerable supporting empirical evidence from both the contemporaneous and historical budget records. Evidence from the contemporaneous record is provided by the budget experience of the tax-financed trust funds. This discussion is deferred to Section 4, where I discuss the issue of trust funds. The historical record, which provides more compelling evidence, is examined in the next section.

The Historical Experience: 1789–1930

In contrast to the years following World War II, the institutional structure of budget decision making in Congress was highly centralized throughout most of the nation's prior fiscal history. From 1789 to 1877, and again from 1922 to the early 1930s, jurisdiction over virtually all spending authority rested with a single committee in each house. Only in the intervening period was this authority widely distributed among congressional committees. A comparison of congressional spending behavior during each of these periods provides the basis for testing the proposition that the post-1930 splintering of spending jurisdiction among congressional committees led to increases in the growth in total government spending irrespective of revenues.

For the first ninety years of the nation's history, almost all spending authority was concentrated in a single committee in each house. From 1789 to 1865, the Ways and Means Committee had jurisdiction over all appropriations in the House. In 1816, the Senate, after briefly experimenting with select committees to handle appropriations, created the Finance Committee as a standing committee with jurisdiction over appropriations. Since these two committees were also the tax-writing committees in each house, the institutional arrangement in these early years can be viewed as consisting of a single "budget" committee responsible for virtually all matters on both sides of the federal budget ledger. In 1865, the House voted to move appropriations jurisdiction from the Ways and Means Committee to a newly created Appropriations Committee. The Senate followed suit two years later and shifted jurisdiction from the Finance Committee to its Appropriations Committee.[18] The shift of jurisdiction over appropriations still left a single congressional committee in each house in charge of all appropriations. This institutional arrangement continued in both houses until 1877.

During the nation's early years, roughly from 1790 to 1835, the desire to liquidate the debt produced a string of almost continuous annual budget surpluses until the Revolutionary War debt was fully extinguished in 1835.[19] After the debt was repaid and before the Civil War, neither surpluses nor deficits persisted for any significant time. The longest string of consecutive budget deficits was the four-year period 1840–43, and the economy suffered through a severe economic recession in the first three of these years.[20] The longest string of consecutive budget surpluses was the eight-year period 1850–57. These surpluses were used to reduce the national debt that had increased greatly during the Mexican-American War.

Following the Civil War, the appropriations committees continued the fiscal restraint practiced by their predecessor committees. Expenditures related to the war effort were cut back sharply, enough so that the income tax was allowed to expire, tariffs were cut, and the war-related debt was reduced by a third.[21]

The year 1877 marked the beginning of a period of radical change in the House of Representatives' procedures regarding spending decisions. The House, in a series of rule changes during the next nine years, stripped the Appropriations Committee of its authority over eight of the fourteen appropriation bills (Fenno, 1966). In each instance, appropriations authority was transferred to the legislative committee that had authorizing jurisdiction over the programs contained in the appropriations bill. In 1877–79, the House Committee on Commerce was allowed to report Rivers and Harbors appropriations directly to the floor, bypassing the Appropriations Committee completely. In 1880, the Agriculture and Forestry Committee was given jurisdiction over the Agriculture Department's appropriations. And in 1883, appropriations for Rivers and Harbors was formally transferred from the Appropriations Committee to a newly created Rivers and Harbors Committee.[22]

The most drastic action, however, occurred in 1885. In that year, jurisdiction for the Army, Consular and Diplomatic, Indian Affairs, Military Academy, Navy, and Post Office and Postal Roads appropriation bills were all transferred from the Appropriations Committee to the various legislative committees. Fourteen years later, the Senate divided appropriations jurisdiction.[23]

The 1885 dispersal of spending authority was without historical precedent. Taken together, the appropriations transferred from the Appropriations Committee constituted almost one-half of all nonmandatory appropriations.[24]

The splintering of appropriations jurisdiction in the House was followed by an upward surge in spending. During the seven years following the House decision, federal program spending grew at a rate unprecedented in the nation's hundred-year history. By 1893, program spending was 50 percent larger than it had been in 1886. The growth of expenditures transformed the 40 percent surplus that existed during 1881–85 into a deficit by 1894. The deficit persisted each year through the remainder of the 1890s. Program expenditures continued their upward march during the years following the Senate decision to divide appropriations jurisdiction in 1899, rising another 45 percent between 1900 and 1916.[25]

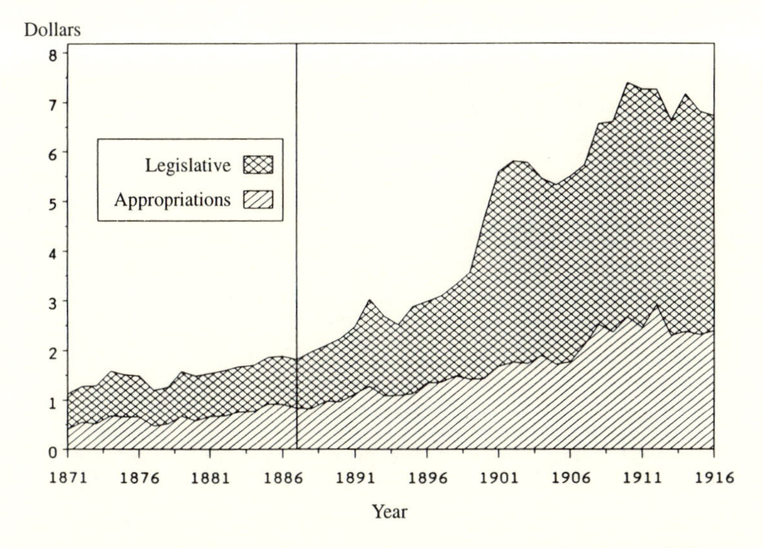

FIGURE 2.4. Impact of Dividing Appropriations Jurisdiction (in billions of FY87 dollars)

The relationship between the growth in federal expenditures and the splintering of spending jurisdiction has been the subject of two recent studies. Brady and Morgan (1987), using aggregate time series data, found a large and statistically significant effect of the dispersal of spending jurisdiction on the growth in spending. In another analysis using more disaggregated data, Stewart (1988) obtained similar results. The following is a more detailed look at the role the division of spending jurisdiction played in contributing to the observed spending increase.

Figure 2.4 shows the trends in appropriations during the period 1871 to 1916. Appropriations during the forty-six years encompassing both the years preceding and following changes in jurisdiction are illustrated. Separate trends are shown for appropriations that remained within the Appropriations Committee jurisdiction and those that were given to the legislating committees.[26] As the graph illustrates, prior to 1887, when the jurisdiction change in the House became effective, funding levels contained in appropriation bills that were subsequently given to the legislative committees (hereafter, legislative committee appropriations) grew at about the

TABLE 2.4
Rivers and Harbors, Agriculture Department, and Legislative Committee Appropriations
($ in thousands)

A. Rivers and Harbors

5-year average	1873–77	1879–83	Percent change
Rivers and Harbors	$5,967	$9,565	60.3%
Total discretionary	$108,984	$107,859	−1.0%

B. Agriculture Department

5-year average	1876–80	1881–85	Percent change
Agriculture Dept.	$194	$380	95.9%
Total discretionary	$96,195	$110,869	15.5%

C. Legislative Committee

5-year average	1882–86	1887–91	Percent growth
Legislative Comm(s).	$47,439	$53,863	13.5%
Appropriations Comm.	$49,668	$53,015	6.7%

SOURCE: U.S. Department of the Treasury, *Digest of Appropriations*, 1939.

same rate (actually at a somewhat slower rate) as those that were retained by the Appropriations Committee.

Immediately following the change in jurisdiction, legislative committee appropriations increased sharply. The Appropriations Committee, on the other hand, continued its prior restraint.

The upward trend in legislating committees' appropriations continued nearly to the end of the century. The size of the change in legislative committee appropriations trend is not trivial. During the ten years prior to the transfer of jurisdiction, the Appropriations Committee cut appropriations for transferred programs at a 5.0 percent annual rate relative to GNP. During the ten years following the transfer, the legislative committees increased appropriations at an annual rate of 1.8 percent.

The Spanish-American War produced a sharp upward surge in legislative committee appropriations. An increase was to be expected since the legislative committees had appropriations jurisdic-

TABLE 2.5

Appropriations Committee vs. Legislative Committees: Appropriation Growth Rates

	30-year growth relative to GNP
Appropriations Committee (1884–1914)	−5.2%
1885 Legislative Committees (1884–1914)	50.0
Rivers and Harbors Committees (1875–1905)	20.7
Agriculture Committee (1878–1908)	1,307.0

SOURCE: *Digest of Appropriations*, 1939. (Computations are based on 5-year moving averages of annual appropriations centered on the years provided in parentheses. Totals exclude all mandatory spending.)

tion over the supply bills for the Army, Navy, and the Military Academy appropriation bills. However, the sharp increase in appropriations between 1898 and 1903 was not limited to those involved exclusively in the war effort. For example, Agriculture Department appropriations increased by 64 percent, Rivers and Harbors by 69 percent, Indian Affairs and Consular and Diplomatic by 17 percent. Following the Spanish-American War, legislative appropriations presumably built up as part of the war effort were cut back to some extent, but not enough to return them to prewar levels.

Table 2.4 provides a more detailed look at the change in appropriation levels that took place immediately following the transfer of jurisdiction. Table 2.4 compares annual appropriations for Rivers and Harbors during the five years preceding the shift in its jurisdiction with the annual appropriations during the five years following the jurisdictional change.[27]

As the data indicate, Rivers and Harbors appropriations jumped by 60 percent during the five years immediately following the transfer of its jurisdiction to the Committee on Commerce. Total appropriations for discretionary programs, in contrast, remained at the same level following the transfer as they were in the years prior to the transfer. The same comparisons for agricultural appropriations and appropriations given to the legislative committees in 1885 tell a similar story.

The long-run cumulative increase in legislative committee appropriations is even more significant. Table 2.5 compares growth rates in appropriations relative to GNP during the thirty years following the House decisions to split jurisdiction. The fiscal restraint practiced by the Appropriations Committee between 1886 and 1916 is indicated by the 5.4 percent decline in its total appropriations relative to GNP during the period. The relative extravagance of the legislative committees is evident from the sizable appropriation growth rates. As a result of these higher growth rates, legislative committee appropriations, which in 1885 were about equal in magnitude to the Appropriations Committee's, exceeded those of the Appropriations Committee by 50 percent thirty years later.

As a result of the rapid growth in the budget, the issue of budgetary process reform gained momentum throughout the years preceding World War I. The issue soon became ripe for the campaign trail. Both political parties recognized the problem and promised to do something about it. The Democratic platform of 1916 called for a return to the pre-1865 single-committee regime: "We demand careful economy in all expenditures and to that end favor a return by the House of Representatives to its former practice of initiating and preparing all appropriation bills through a single committee."[28]

The Republican party platform was less explicit. It called for enactment of former President Taft's "oft-repeated and earnest proposal efforts to secure economy and efficiency through the establishment of a single and business-like budget system."[29]

President Wilson, himself a student of Congress, joined those calling for budget process reform in his 1917 State of the Union message following his election to a second term:

> And I beg that the members of the House of Representatives will permit me to express the opinion that it will be impossible to deal in any but a very wasteful and extravagant fashion with the enormous appropriations of public moneys . . . unless the House will consent to return to its former practice of initiating and preparing all appropriation bills through a single committee.[30]

World War I temporarily diverted attention from the issue of budget process reform. But as soon as the war ended, the reform effort was immediately taken up again. In October 1919, a select committee on the budget was established and submitted its report to the Congress later in the year. The centerpiece of the report was a recommendation that the House adopt a resolution that "centers in one Committee on Appropriations . . . the authority to report all appropriations."[31] According to the committee, effective control over the budget could not be achieved without consolidating spending jurisdiction. As the committee report summarized: "Without the adoption of this resolution true budgetary reform is impossible."[32]

The Select Committee knew it was proposing a dramatic step. Never before in the history of the Congress had authority been stripped away from so many committees. However, the committee also knew that the wide distribution of spending jurisdiction was not in the general interest. "While it [the resolution] means the surrender by certain committees of jurisdiction which they now possess and will take from certain members on those committees certain powers now exercised, we ought to approach the consideration of the big problem with a determination to submerge personal ambition for the public good."[33]

The day the House Select Committee on the Budget submitted its recommendations, it also reported out a bill to implement them.[34] The bill, authored by the Select Committee's chairman, James W. Good, sent shock waves reverberating through legislative committee hearing rooms. It proposed that the House wrench appropriations authority from seven powerful legislative committees.

More than seven months elapsed before the resolution was brought to the House floor.[35] By the time it came to the floor, a majority had been marshaled in its favor, and the resolution passed by a vote of 200–117.[36]

There were undoubtedly many reasons for the House action. The overriding one, though, was a belief that without it, fiscal restraint could not be achieved. Still, it is not clear that budget economy arguments alone would have carried the day in the House. Also important was the fact that the resolution had previously been embraced in almost identical form by the Democratic party platform and was consistent with the thrust of the Republican party's platform. During the floor debate on the consolidation bill, several members reminded the Democratic members of this fact, but none as forcefully as James Good. In a powerful statement, Good began by invoking the words of former party leader William Jennings

TABLE 2.6
Federal Spending and Budget Surpluses, 1920s
($ in billions)

	Outlays	Surplus	Percent of GNP Outlays	Percent of GNP Surplus
1920	$3.3	$0.7	4.6%	1.0%
1924	2.9	1.0	3.4	1.1
1926	2.9	0.9	3.0	0.9
1928	3.0	0.9	3.1	0.9
1930	3.3	0.7	3.4	0.7

SOURCE: U.S. Dept. of the Treasury *Annual Report*, 1980.

Bryan on the importance of adhering to the platform. "The Representative who secures office on a platform and then betrays the people who elected him is a criminal worse than he who embezzles money." Good then reminded his fellow Democrats that an election was five months away: "A real test has come, vote to repudiate your platform or vote to carry out its provisions. But I want to assure you those Democrats who vote to repudiate their platform in this respect will, I believe, live to regret that action, and your desserts may come sooner than you think."[37]

The Senate followed the House two years later. On March 6, 1922, the Senate amended its rules to provide that all appropriation bills should be considered by one committee instead of many.[38]

The years following the consolidation of spending authority in the House and Senate was a period of remarkable fiscal restraint. During the 1920s, the almost unbroken upward march of government spending of the preceding three decades was halted. The budget was in surplus each year from 1920 to 1930, and the size of the budget surplus actually increased from the beginning of the decade to its end.

Table 2.6 summarizes the budget expenditures and surpluses for the decade. The aggregate data for this brief ten-year period are compelling. The year 1922 marks the end of the natural wind-down of federal expenditures following World War I.[39] From that year to the beginning of the decade, federal expenditures remained virtually unchanged. Relative to GNP, the decade of the 1920s witnessed a reversal of prior decade increases in government spending.

The eleven-year string of consecutive budget surpluses from 1920 to 1930 was the longest since the 1880s, when the spending authority was dispersed in the House.

The Behavior of Trust-Fund Budgets

The Social Security Act created the first tax-financed trust fund, the Old Age Survivors Insurance Trust Fund. Prior to the passage of the Social Security Act in 1935, no major tax-financed trust fund existed in the federal budget. In contrast to general-fund programs, jurisdiction over expenditures for each of the tax-financed trust funds resides with a single committee (see Table 2.7). This difference provides a natural test for the importance of the dispersal-of-spending-authority hypothesis. If the thesis of this paper is correct, we should expect to observe no persistent deficits in the trust funds.

With the exception of the Railroad Retirement fund, the individual tax-financed trust funds have all avoided running persistent deficits. The extent to which they have is provided by the summary statistics on each of the trust funds in Table 2.8.

As the data indicate, although each of the trust funds (again with the exception of the Railroad Retirement fund) has at times run deficits, these deficits have been few in number and do not persist for any significant time.[40] Most of the deficits have occurred during years of economic contraction. In these years, the decline in economic activity produces a sharp falloff in trust-fund revenues. As the economy recovers, so do trust revenues, and the fund re-

TABLE 2.7

Major Tax-Financed Trust Funds

Program	House committee with spending jurisdiction
Old-Age Survivors Insurance (1935)	Ways and Means
Railroad Retirement (1936)	Ways and Means
Social Security Disability Insurance (1956)	Ways and Means
Highways (1956)[a]	Public Works
Medicare Hospital Insurance (1965)	Ways and Means
Airport and Airways (1970)[a]	Public Works

SOURCE: Committee on Ways and Means, 1988.
[a]Jurisdiction is shared with the Appropriations Committee.

TABLE 2.8

Selected Performance Indicators of Tax-Financed Trust Funds, 1935–89

	Years in operation	Years in deficit	Longest string of consecutive deficits
Social Security (OASI) (1935)	53	14	8
Railroad Retirement (1937)	55	32	32
Disability Insurance (1956)	35	13	4
Highway Trust Fund (1956)	36	10	3
Medicare (Part A) (1965)	26	1	1
Airports and Airways (1970)	22	3	2

SOURCE: *Budget*, 1952–89, Annual Reports of the Secretary of the Treasury, 1941–51. (Dates in parenthesis are the dates of enactment of the programs.) Years in operation refers to the number of years in which payments have been made from the fund.

turns to surplus.[41] The financial behavior of the trust funds is strikingly similar to that of the total budget in the nineteenth century, when spending jurisdiction was highly concentrated.

The creation of tax-financed trust funds did not have a neutral effect on the budget deficit. Quite the contrary. The trust funds, because of the way they were financed and the incentives they created for the tax-writing committees, produced significant downward pressure on general-fund revenues.

When the Social Security trust fund was created, the issue of the appropriate method of financing the fund's expected long-term expenditures arose. The Social Security program's architects recognized that the program's costs would rise as the program matured. To finance the expected rise in costs, two options were available.[42] The first was to set the tax necessary to finance the long-run costs at a constant level over the life of the program. This option would generate surplus revenues early in the program's development. The surplus could be used later to defray the higher costs as the program matured. The second option was to schedule a series of increases in taxes so that revenues would rise in step with the program's costs.[43] After a brief experiment with the first option, the tax-writing committees settled on the second. The same basic decision was made for each of the trust funds, but especially important were those whose future costs were expected to rise: Disability Insurance and Medicare.

Adoption of this rule meant that the tax-writing committees

TABLE 2.9
Trust-Fund Taxes vs. General-Fund Taxes
(as a percent of GNP)

	1950–54	1960–64	1970–74	1980–84	1990–92
Trust Fund	1.0%	2.9%	4.6%	5.8%	6.9%
General Fund	16.3	14.8	13.5	12.9	11.5

SOURCE: *Budget*, various years. (Trust-fund taxes include OASI, DI, Medicare (HI), Highway trust-fund, and Airport trust-fund taxes. General-fund taxes include all other taxes except state unemployment insurance taxes.)

would have to finance the trust funds and the general fund on the same basis: current taxes for current benefits. Adoption of this rule also meant that payroll tax increases would necessarily have to be built into certain trust funds (Social Security, Disability Insurance, and Medicare). A consequence of the automatic tax increases built into one fund would naturally be downward pressure on taxes in the other fund.

The introduction of a tax bias compounded the problem. There were two sources for this bias. Benefits of trust expenditures could be specifically identified and were directly tied to the revenues raised, but general expenditures were more diffuse, ranging from national defense to nutrition programs. The greater ability to identify the direct benefits of any trust-fund tax hike made trust-fund taxes less painful to raise.

The second source of bias resulted from placing jurisdiction over expenditures for the Social Security Act programs in the tax-writing committees. This meant that allocating the proceeds of Social Security Act taxes would be in the hands of the tax-writing committees. Allocating the proceeds of general taxes, on the other hand, would be determined by at least a dozen other committees. If taxes had to be raised, the tax-writing committees would naturally tend to favor the former.

Table 2.9 shows the combined impact of these forces on trust and general revenues during the post–World War II years. The table displays revenues as a percent of GNP for five-year intervals during each decade. From each decade to the next, trust revenues rise, and general revenues decline. The growth in the former each decade is only slightly greater than the decline in the latter. It is almost as if there were a dollar-for-dollar substitution of trust for general revenues relative to GNP. The rise in trust revenues seems to be crowding out general revenues.

Summary and Conclusions

The central thesis of this chapter has been that two key institutional changes occurring in the Congress during the last fifty years have contributed importantly to the emergence of a structural federal budget deficit. The division of spending authority among numerous committees created upward pressure on general-fund expenditures. The enactment of major tax-financed trust funds simultaneously produced downward pressure on general-fund revenues. Evidence that supports this thesis has been found both in the budget patterns following the nineteenth-century decision by the House of Representatives to divide spending authority and in the balance between expenditures and revenues in the trust funds.

This chapter, however, has provided only a partial explanation for the budget deficits. Many questions remain unanswered. For example, the institutional arrangements employed by the Congress are undoubtedly influenced by the desire to facilitate a particular outcome. Thus, one remaining and rather fundamental question is why the institutional changes occurred? To what extent were these changes simply a mechanism used to facilitate an increase in the rate of spending? Why were the particular forms of institutional change adopted? Also, this chapter has not addressed the role of the President in the budget process. Yet, through the power to propose, the bully pulpit, and the power to veto, the President can obviously wield an enormous influence over fiscal outcomes. The President's role in the process needs to be given an explicit treatment in future work.

3

The Uses and Abuses of Budget Baselines

TIMOTHY J. MURIS

THROUGH the 1980s, Congress and the executive branch claimed that they had cut the deficit in the federal budget by tens of billions of dollars. In October 1990, those responsible for the budget made their largest claims to date: a deficit reduction for the years 1991–95 of nearly $500 billion. Yet the deficits for 1991 and 1992 are the highest ever recorded.* This phenomenon holds for individual programs. In the last decade, for example, Medicare reductions were said to exceed $50 billion. Yet from 1979 through 1989, Medicare outlays more than tripled, from $29 billion to $94 billion.[1] In the 1990 budget summit, large cuts in Medicare were again claimed, yet Medicare will grow from $114 billion in 1991 to $173 billion in 1995.[2] Similar facts obtain with regard to federal pay. During the Reagan administration, civilian federal employees received an average annual salary increase of about 3 percent. Yet billions of dollars in alleged deficit reduction resulted from "cutting" federal pay. National defense provides still another example: despite large increases in defense spending in the 1980s, billions of dollars were claimed in deficit reduction. In August 1985, for example, Congress's budget resolution allowed a defense appropriation of $303 billion, an increase of $8 billion above the previous year's appropriation. Yet Congress claimed that it was saving $22 billion.

What explains these apparent anomalies? The answer is that

*Unless otherwise indicated, all years in this chapter are fiscal years.

these claims of deficit reduction are made against "baselines," not actual outlays or receipts. Baselines are projections of budget outcomes; reductions and increases are calculated from these projections, not from actual revenues or expenditures. Begun in the mid-1970s and at first resisted in some quarters, the use of baselines in all budget discussions prevailed by the early 1980s. As we will see, these baselines confuse press and public alike, allowing those in power to claim significant reductions in the deficit while actually adopting increases.

This chapter considers the origins, uses, and abuses of budget baselines. It argues that one of the original purposes of baselines, to estimate "current services"—that is, what it would cost tomorrow to provide today's government—has not been, and indeed could not be, implemented in practice. Instead, there is a system in place to discuss budget matters that is understood by only a few budget technicians. To people ignorant of this system's rules, a spending increase can be a cut, a tax increase may not be an increase, and the maturing of a major new program counts as part of current spending and not an increase, even though when fully implemented it will cost billions more than when first passed.

In the next section I consider the origins of the baseline concept and explain the different baselines used. In later sections I discuss why current services cannot be calculated in practice, the many ways the baseline actually employed—so-called current policy—is used, and the impact of using current policy. The last section discusses alternatives to current policy.

The Rise and Evolution of Baselines

Throughout most of U.S. history, the base used to compare alternative budget proposals was either the levels in the previous year's budget or those proposed by the President. Beginning with the Congressional Budget Act of 1974, more elaborate bases, called baselines, came into play. The act required a baseline that continued current programs at "the same level as the current year without a change in policy."[3] This baseline was intended to provide a policy-neutral method to project accurately what it would cost in the future to continue government as it exists today. Such a baseline, it was felt, would be better for assessing the fiscal impact of new proposals than the cruder measures previously used.

How to define the baseline was unclear, however, and the legislative history gave no precise guidance. Alternative definitions developed. One possibility is to measure a constant level of government services to determine if a proposed change would increase or decrease government. This view uses as a baseline "current services," meaning a measure of what it would cost in the future to provide the services the government provides today. Other definitions focus on the words "without a change in policy." Under this approach, the baseline should put the government on "automatic pilot," and determine how much it would cost to fund it in the future if no new legislation were passed.[4] This view is called "current policy."[5] A third alternative is called "current law." It differs from "current policy" in not including adjustments for inflation of discretionary spending.

Appendix B explores the legislative history of the baseline requirement and explains the technical differences between baseline concepts. This chapter details the impossibility of a true measure of current services and the manipulations that occur in the baseline actually used. Which baseline to use was debated throughout the 1970s. Not until the 1982 budget process was the issue resolved, a resolution that continues today.*

In preparing baselines under the 1974 Budget Act, neither OMB nor CBO attempted to calculate true current services, with limited exceptions, because for many programs "literally measuring a current level of services . . . would be extremely burdensome, conceptually meaningless, or both."[6] OMB began by using current law, although it provided a separate adjustment to show the overall impact of adding provisions for inflation adjustments of discretionary spending. In fiscal 1980, OMB provided for inflation of defense spending only; after being criticized for inconsistency, it inflated all discretionary programs the next year. CBO inflated discretionary spending, but also included separate current law estimates.

Of the two Congressional budget committees, the House committee did not use the baseline concept in the Budget Act until the Reagan administration. The Senate Budget Committee began by

*Although the general issue has been resolved, the details of particular estimates still occasionally change. For example, over much of the 1980s, increases in the defense "baseline" exceeded the general inflation rate, which was intended mainly to provide more money for defense while claiming higher "savings" when the totals were announced.

using current policy, claiming it was policy-neutral. Faced with protests from the Ford administration, which had proposed spending far less than current policy, Senator Edmund Muskie (D-Maine) used current policy to argue that Congress, which desired to spend more than the administration, actually was "cutting" the budget, not increasing it. Concern over the meaning and nature of current policy led the Senate Budget Committee to use both current policy and current law. By the end of the Carter administration, the Senate Budget Committee relied primarily on current law, although information was provided on possible inflation and workload increases.[7]

Thus, on the eve of the Reagan administration, current policy, which showed spending growing faster than current law (since it adjusted for inflation), did not yet hold sway. Although preferred by budget technicians at both CBO and OMB, it was not used in the House and was losing credibility in the Senate. The yearly ritual of the 1980s, with large "deficit reduction" packages based on current policy, had not yet taken shape. All this changed in the Reagan administration. In submissions to Congress in early 1981, the administration claimed a deficit reduction of $48.6 billion.[8] These "cuts" were from a current policy baseline that had been adjusted to provide for "adequate" defense, with *adequate* defined to exceed the general inflation rate. There were comparisons to previous absolute levels, as well as to the absolute levels outgoing President Carter had proposed, but the emphasis was on reductions from projections, not on absolute reductions in programs or in the deficit compared to deficits of previous years. Press accounts emphasized the size of the proposed "cuts,"[9] although most did mention the year-to-year changes. For example, the lead story in the *New York Times* used words like "cut" and "cutback" twenty times, and mentioned that the annual growth of outlays would "slow" to 7 percent only in the story's last paragraph on page B9.[10]

The current policy baseline has become the dominant measure used for evaluating and reporting on budget proposals. The Budget summit agreement reached between President Reagan and Congress on November 20, 1987, is revealing. The *entire* presentation of the deficit reduction provisions was given in terms of changes from the baseline. Not only were absolute receipt, outlay, and deficit numbers not presented to the public; they were not even considered during the summit negotiations.[11] In the budget summit of late 1990, the negotiators focused on achieving a $500 billion reduction from current policy over five years that, coupled with optimistic economic assumptions, would eliminate the budget deficit. The package was routinely described as a "five-year, $500 billion deficit reduction."

Although current policy is the measure currently in use, it is still often called current services and defended as providing a good estimate of how much it would cost tomorrow to pay for today's government, i.e., of current services.[12] We turn next to the question of accurately measuring current services.

The Chimera of Current Services

A baseline that projects the cost of the current level of all government activities into the future is an illusion. There are two major problems. First, events outside the congressional spending process can change the funding level needed to hold government constant. In other words, tomorrow's government can require, because of events outside its control, more or less money than today's to provide the same services. The second reason is that, even discounting such exogenous events, determining what amounts will be necessary to fund government at a constant level is a complex matter. As we shall see, simple formulas such as adjusting all discretionary programs for inflation can fail to measure accurately a constant level of government. Many variables can influence the calculus, and even when current services for a particular program are carefully calculated, experts may reasonably disagree over the correct estimate, thus undermining the supposed policy neutrality and objectivity of the current services baseline.

Exogenous Events

National defense provides a prime example of the way exogenous events influence spending needs. The money spent on defense presumably purchases security for the people of the United States. How secure we are cannot be determined independently of the threats we face. With the decline in the Soviet threat, the amount needed to protect us has decreased. Although there is no doubt that the armed forces of the United States will be substantially reduced as a result of the Soviet collapse, the basic policy remains constant. That is, Congress and the Executive have not decided to make the United States less secure; rather, less money is needed to provide the same security.

Regulatory agencies provide other examples of the ways decisions outside the congressional funding process influence the level of spending needed to hold government constant. When Congress delegates to regulatory agencies the discretion to implement laws, the amount required to fund a constant level of government depends upon the policies the regulators follow.

Consider the Antitrust Division of the Department of Justice. Under President Reagan the division favored a narrower interpretation of antitrust laws than previous administrations. Big cases against alleged single-firm monopolies, such as IBM, were dropped. Cases against vertical integration practices and conglomerate mergers were halted. Other activities, such as criminal prosecutions, were increased, but the net result allowed the division's mission to be performed with many fewer people. Inflating Carter administration levels, the amount the current policy baseline would have claimed as current services, would have significantly overstated the resources needed to maintain the division's program. In fact, as with defense spending in recent years, expenditures declined from previous levels. But using last year as the base was supposedly a crude device, over which current services would be an improvement!

Consumer protection at the Federal Trade Commission (FTC) provides another example. During the second half of the 1970s, many expensive proceedings were held to promulgate command-and-control regulations for entire industries. Because the Reagan administration abandoned this undertaking, the FTC's consumer protection program required less money. Again, an inflation adjustment would have been irrelevant. The same story could be repeated for many regulatory agencies during the 1980s.

One might object that these shifts were policy changes, and hence reflecting them in current services would be inconsistent with a policy-neutral baseline. Of course policy changed, but the change had nothing to do with a congressional funding decision. When regulators have a high degree of discretion, the funding they need can *only* be determined by the policy they currently follow. The policy-neutral baseline is thus an illusion. To claim that current services required the Carter administration level plus inflation would have meant giving these agencies much greater funding than they needed for *their* current programs.

Another event exogenous to congressional spending decisions is the accomplishment of a program's objectives. To hold government activity constant, sensitivity to the purposes of programs is required. If the original purpose of a program is achieved, yet spending continues for a new purpose, then government involvement in the economy has increased, not remained constant. For example, early in the Carter administration, Congress increased job-training funding in response to a recession. Once the recession ended, continuing the program meant an increase in government activity.

General revenue sharing provides a similar example. The program was created because of the poor fiscal condition of many state and local governments. As the federal deficit increased, states and localities began to run surpluses. Measured against a constant level of federal government involvement in the economy, continuing the program would thus have *increased* government, with spending used for a new purpose.

Similarly, a program whose purposes are fulfilled at lower than the anticipated cost does not mean a reduction in government activity. For example, Title III of the Job Training Partnership Act, passed in 1982, proved to have an actual cost per person roughly half that originally foreseen. A decrease in spending to that level would not decrease government.[13]

Current Services for Discretionary Programs

Discretionary programs are reviewed and funded annually. Current policy simply inflates last year's level, usually by the projected GNP deflator, on the assumption that this adjustment produces a good estimate of what it will cost to provide the same level of services for another year. To determine if such adjustments are a reliable proxy for current services even in the absence of exogenous events, we will distinguish programs that fund purchases, such as aircraft carriers, dams, or space vehicles, from programs that fund employees, such as the regulatory and law enforcement agencies, as well as the rest of the government's bureaucracy.

Purchases. When government commits to large purchases, current services implies all funds necessary to complete and use the investment.* For example, once the government contracts for a building, the cost of completing the building should be included in the baseline. National defense presents a more complicated case. Defense includes expenditures for paying soldiers, procuring equipment ranging from boots and rifles to multibillion-dollar aircraft carriers, providing support services to maintain and operate this equipment, constructing and maintaining military facilities, and engaging in research and development for new generations of weapons. At any time, the recent appropriations of Congress give us a picture—of more or less clarity, depending on the degree of controversy over decisions—of an overall defense program. An accurate measure of current services must include all the costs of implementing that program. For example, if, as in the early 1980s, Congress increases the number of aircraft carriers planned to fifteen, this decision influences the rest of the Navy's budget. More sailors must be recruited to run the ships, more plans must be procured to take off from them, more ships are needed to support the new carriers, and more money is required to operate and maintain the larger fleet. Such an expansion requires adjusting previous levels by an amount greater than inflation.

As circumstances change, so do "current services" requirements. For example, at the end of a massive procurement buildup, less money will be needed to operate the weapons than was needed to buy them. Moreover, just as Congress may decide to increase the size of the armed forces, it may decide to decrease them, thereby decreasing the cost of continuing current services. As ships become obsolete, for example, Congress may decide to retire rather than replace them.

But how do we know what the congressionally approved defense program is? With aircraft carriers, the answer is easy. Congress fully funds carriers, giving the Pentagon in the first year all the budget authority necessary to build the ship even though it takes

*Under narrow circumstances, OMB has deviated from simple inflation adjustments for construction projects. *See* OMB Circular A-11, pp. 63–64. CBO has deviated in the past as well, although less frequently than OMB.

years before all the money is paid out. Once this commitment is made, the personnel, ships, planes, and operating funds needed to support the carrier all become part of current services.

What services currently are is often unclear, however. It is not always possible to know what a congressional decision is. Consider the National Aeronautics and Space Administration. By the end of the Reagan administration, NASA, its advisory committees, and the industries it affects envisioned a core program that required a budget increase over five years of more than 50 percent, measured in constant dollars.[14] Although its authorization committees supported this program, Congress as a whole may have disagreed. NASA based the need for increased funding in part on increased cost estimates for meeting its goals, in part because its plans extend its emphasis on manned space flight, in part because of the perceived spin-off benefits from investment in NASA projects. Yet given yearly review of the program in Congress, possible extensions in the time allowed to accomplish goals, and lack of agreement on objectives, picking the services that are current is difficult indeed.

As discussed above, defense current services cannot be automatically calculated. Besides the policy issue of what level of forces is needed given the diminished Soviet threat, other issues make the calculation problematic. Once the size of the forces and the numbers and kinds of weapons to be used are determined, Congress must decide how much operations and support costs are needed to maintain them. The decision cannot be made mechanically. Thus in 1988, CBO published a report addressing this issue, concluding that there were three different methods of estimating operations and support costs, each of them reasonable.[15] One method, projecting support costs based on force size, would have required $35 billion less in constant 1988 dollars through 1992 than an estimate based on a capital stock model, which assumes that operations and support costs are related to the dollar value of the stock of equipment operated. The administration projected operations and support costs to increase at a rate roughly halfway between the other two methods. Thus, even when the difficult issue of which force levels and weapons Congress has actually approved is addressed, reasonable estimates of the true support costs still vary by tens of billions of dollars.

Grants to state and local governments also show the difficulty of determining what current services means. One budget official defended applying an inflation adjustment rather than calculating current services for general revenue sharing because the money "went to communities throughout the United States and was available for use for a wide variety of purposes. Measuring the actual level of services provided by general revenue sharing funds and projecting their future costs seemed to be a monumentally difficult task."[16]

These examples are hardly isolated. With discretionary accounts, decisions are made each year only to be reevaluated the next. Many decisions are compromises, leaving the issue to be resolved another day. Given the many voices in Congress and frequently changing coalitions, it could hardly be otherwise. In such an environment, determining what services are indeed current is often impossible.

People programs. For many programs, the primary expenditure is on government employees, and it is as difficult to judge what services are current in these programs as in procurement programs. As explained above, the true current level of services depends upon the changing nature of the mission performed. In a stable environment, services would be maintained at current levels by funding the current number of people, less improvements for productivity. But the environment is not always stable. The preceding discussion of the defense budget applies to the more than $75 billion spent annually on military personnel.[17] The decision to purchase more or fewer ships, for example, affects the number of sailors needed. Moreover, to the extent that our allies increase or decrease their forces, the size of U.S. military forces needed to keep the level of defense "current" will change. With domestic agencies, the issues are similar, often requiring difficult calculations to determine the current services level of employees.

One problem with mechanical inflation increases for discretionary accounts is the failure to account for changes in productivity. Many areas of government have had sharp productivity increases. In the Carter and Reagan years, for example, the Social Security Administration reduced its workforce by 10 percent while its caseload increased about 20 percent. In 1977 the Social Security Administration had one employee for every 432 beneficiaries; by 1986 it had one employee for every 536.[18] Moreover, personal computers and advanced word processors have greatly increased the productivity of clerical and professional workers. For example, the cost of producing legal papers has decreased through word processing and through the computerization of various research tools.*

The problem of policy judgment. Thus far, we have focused on the difficulty of calculating true current services. Even when proxies can be developed, they cannot be calculated mechanically. To continue our defense example, disagreement exists on how much funding is needed under the current defense program. Estimates vary widely among experts, with the Bush administration favoring higher amounts than many in Congress.[19] Not surprisingly, the differences reflect, to a considerable extent, different views on the defense policies the United States should follow. Although current services can be estimated under this uncertainty, reasonable people will differ. To choose among the reasonable estimates requires favoring one policy view over another.

To those who construct the baseline, particularly in CBO, judgments on policy present great difficulties. The staff of CBO perceive the baseline as policy-neutral and themselves as objective and nonpartisan. CBO's baseline projections and estimates of the cost of legislation often determine the fate of program proposals. CBO estimates are the starting point for program analysis and the ending point in determining whether proposals exceed the allocations of the congressional budget resolution. Thus, the CBO baseline is hardly an academic matter. CBO constructs its baselines primarily with formulas—e.g., it inflates discretionary programs by the general inflation rate—to avoid confrontations with members of Congress. Such mechanical calculation avoids the lobbying that would otherwise occur each year to determine which of the competing reasonable estimates of current services should in fact be used for various programs. Indeed, CBO's independence would be threatened if it could not avoid, or at least minimize, such controversies.†

*OMB has attempted to adjust for productivity increases in agencies on an ad hoc basis, primarily through the device of "absorption." The baseline would not increase by the full amount of any pay increase, as agencies were assumed to "absorb" part of the additional funding for pay.

†The dispute in the 1980s between the House and the Senate over naming a new director of CBO, a post that was vacant for two years, provides some indication of the sensitivity of CBO's position. The *Washington Post* ran an editorial on Nov. 4,

In programs with no clear level of current services, CBO would have to choose between competing measurements to calculate the baseline, necessarily offending those who disagree with its decision.

One might object that even the formulas CBO uses require judgment with considerable policy implications. For example, the formula for discretionary programs requires estimates of future inflation rates, which in turn require considerable skill and judgment to reach. This point is valid, but CBO minimizes political problems by adopting forecasts close to the consensus of private forecasters. Indeed, such a consensus forecast is routinely published and is widely discussed in the financial press.[20] The existence of such a consensus forecast gives CBO's projections legitimacy. No such consensus exists for most of the other judgments necessary to calculate current services accurately.*

Current Services for Mandatory Programs

Mandatory programs constitute a growing share of government expenditures. Only 29 percent of noninterest outlays in 1965, by 1990 mandatory programs had grown to nearly 50 percent of such outlays.[21] Although the problems here differ from those posed by discretionary programs, a proper calculation of current services—the cost tomorrow of providing today's government—cannot be done mechanically or easily for many programs.

In March 1990, CBO published a staff memorandum that lists the five largest sources of projected growth in spending from the

---

1987, noting the concern in some quarters over the alleged desire of the House for a more politically oriented director. Although the career staff of OMB are as neutral and objective as those of CBO, judgments about competing reasonable alternatives may be easier for OMB to reach, because it is managed by an administration with an explicit policy agenda. But this very fact is the main reason why CBO's baseline is used more frequently. The procedures of the 1990 budget summit appear to make OMB estimates more important than those of CBO, but at least in the House, CBO will continue to be used. See, e.g., "Parties Wrangle," *Congressional Quarterly*, Dec. 8, 1990, at 4072.

*At the request of the Senate Budget Committee, for a brief time CBO did attempt to calculate "true" current services for defense. In part because of the Reagan administration's desire to increase defense spending, the committee asked CBO to use a baseline with higher adjustments than inflation. Faced with increasing controversy over this baseline, CBO eventually abandoned it.

1990 levels: increases in entitlement program caseloads, rising outlays for new Social Security beneficiaries, cost-of-living adjustments for entitlement programs, increases in costs of medical care, and increases in use of medical care.[22] Of the five, which should be considered "true" current services and incorporated into CBO's baseline? To exclude the increase in caseloads would result in a reduction in services per individual. For this reason, the cost tomorrow of providing today's government should include caseload growth; otherwise, services per individual would drop.

What about the amounts new Social Security beneficiaries will receive in excess of the amounts that recently deceased recipients received? Whether this amount should be included as current services depends upon whether one believes current services automatically includes the promise to pay greater average benefits in the future. These rises in benefits are certainly a part of current law, and hence are easily justified as being in the current policy baseline. But this conclusion does not tell us whether paying higher average benefits is increasing today's government or maintaining it. Similarly, the cost-of-living adjustment provides larger checks to recipients, and in this sense could be considered an increase in the cost of government, not provision of current services. Nevertheless, because the cost-of-living adjustment is meant to hold purchasing power constant, it is frequently defended as keeping the benefits to individuals "current."

The last two sources of increase cited in the CBO memorandum involve medical care. Both the increase in the cost of medical care and an increase in its use have dramatically increased spending projections. (The CBO memorandum estimated that medical inflation would add $85 billion to the baseline from 1991 to 1995, and that increased use would add another $179 billion.) Here, the difficulty in calculating current services is greater still. Three Medicare problems illustrate the difficulties in calculating current services for medical programs. The first involves the services held current. To calculate current services, we should adjust the services patients currently receive for inflation and allow for an increase in the number of beneficiaries. From 1981 to 1986, for example, Medicare spending increased 79 percent. The number of Medicare beneficiaries increased 12 percent, and the Consumer Price Index increased

21 percent. Thus, 46 percentage points of the growth cannot be explained by general inflation or increases in the number of beneficiaries. Inflation for medical care in general, however, was 48 percent from 1980 to 1986. Even if we accept the medical inflation rate as the appropriate index, 19 percentage points of Medicare growth is not explained by inflation and an increased number of beneficiaries.

Moreover, the reasons for the rapid growth in medical costs are relevant to defining current services. As is now well understood, the normal cost-control incentives that work in most markets are weakened with respect to health care because most people receiving services do not directly pay for them. Hospitals and doctors have both financial and legal incentives to increase the frequency and intensity with which they examine and treat patients, providing them with more services, such as expensive tests, per visit. Were patients bearing the full cost, they would have a greater incentive to weigh those costs against estimates of their probable benefit. A large body of theoretical and empirical literature shows that reducing the incentive to make a cost-benefit calculation causes medical costs to accelerate rapidly.[23]

Medicare spending on physicians' services provides dramatic evidence of this pattern. From 1980 to 1985, such spending grew by 16 percent a year. In fiscal 1986, during a Congressional "freeze" on physicians' fees, spending grew 8.5 percent, although the number of beneficiaries increased only 2 percent. By contrast, hospital spending increases have recently slowed,[24] reflecting legislation that reduced the incentives to overprovide services. Nevertheless, even with hospitals, there is dramatic evidence of increased costs in response to the system's incentives. In 1988, for example, the increase in cost per hospital case from the aging of the population and the treatment of more complex illnesses was 0.5 percent. According to the Department of Health and Human Services, the increase in cost per case from the manner in which hospitals *classified* illnesses was *three times* higher. Thus, over time, hospitals have charged Medicare more for treating the same illness by recategorizing the illness as a more complex one.

These problems are brought home by the $264 billion increases in the use and price of medical care that CBO estimated for their 1991–95 baseline. These components of the baseline largely reflect not funds needed to provide *current* services, but funds needed for *increased* services.*

The technicians preparing current policy estimates assume that Medicare will continue its rapid expansion unless there are statutory or regulatory changes to reduce the rate of growth. They explicitly assume that medical services will *increase.* To compile an estimate of the actual cost tomorrow of maintaining current health care would require discounting for the behavior of providers and patients. Paying for the levels of high-cost services the system encourages is paying for more than is necessary to maintain care at current levels. Thus, the extraordinary growth in medical services is in part an artifact of the system's distorted incentives.

Simply using the general inflation rate and eliminating the increased use of medical care from the baseline, however, would not necessarily provide a correct estimate for current services. One problem is that the population is gradually aging, increasing medical problems per beneficiary, and making more services necessary to maintain health. An additional problem involves changing medical technology. As medical science evolves, new, sometimes very costly techniques to treat illnesses are developed. The medicine of 1990 is superior to that of 1980, and some of the increased costs of Medicare reflect this superiority. But is this superiority a "current service"?

Another problem in defining current services for Medicare involves annual increases in certain payments. For example, beginning in 1984 Congress began paying hospitals under the prospective payment system (PPS), based on the diagnosis of the patients' illness, not on the services they actually receive. Each year the PPS payment scale is increased or "updated." This update, once set by the Secretary of Health and Human Services, is congressionally mandated. It is supposed to be based on several variables, including input inflation (called the "market basket"), hospital practice patterns, and hospital productivity.[25] The actual update has usually been below increases in the market basket. For example, the average 1988 update of about 38 percent of the increases in market

*The word "largely" reflects two facts. First, some part of the inflation adjustment *is* part of current services. Second, CBO did not estimate the impact of improved medical technology. Such improvements can decrease, as well as increase, costs.

basket and the average 1989 update of about 60 percent of market basket increases far exceeded past updates.*

One reason the updates tended to be far below the increase in the market basket was the realization that the original base upon which the PPS formula was set overcompensated hospitals. Although average profit margins were zero before the change, they grew to 15 percent in 1984 and 1985. The Health and Human Services Inspector General, the GAO, and OMB concluded that "rebasing" the system would end the overcompensation, thereby significantly lowering hospital payments.[26] Nevertheless, the current policy baseline uses the full increase in the market basket. Although the market basket yields a formula and thus avoids policy judgment, by the standards of past practice it exceeds current services.

Using the market basket also illustrates the final problem in calculating the Medicare baseline, failure to account for changes in hospital productivity. By contrast, physician productivity is included to a limited extent. Medicare payments for physicians are limited to the charges that prevailed in 1973 updated for the change in physician practice costs as reflected by the Medicare Economic Index (MEI). One part of the MEI, accounting for about 40 percent, measures changes in the prices physicians pay for the goods and services they need to operate their practice. No allowance is made for changes in productivity. The rest of the MEI, however, increases by physician income, reflecting changes in productivity as measured by the index of output per person hour of nonfarm workers. Because about half of all physicians who see patients charge at the limits MEI allows, current policy projections of physician payments do reflect a part of the increases in productivity.[27] In some areas, however, there have been significant increases in productivity, cataract surgery being a prime example. Once very complex, delicate, and time-consuming, technical improvements have reduced its cost drastically. Payment for cataract surgery, as well as

*The 1990 and 1991 urban updates were 85 percent and 62 percent of the market basket, respectively. In 1990, large urban hospitals received an update almost at the level of market basket increase and rural hospitals received an update well above it. In 1991, rural hospitals received an update of 4.5 percent, 0.7 percent below the market basket. For a general explanation of the operation of the PPS system, see U.S. Congress, CBO, *Including Capital Expenses*, Appendix, Aug. 1988.

other so-called overpriced procedures, was not reformed until recently, however, and thus was included in the baseline without reflecting increased productivity.[28] Moreover, despite the improved technology and patient outcomes, the reform was called a "cut" in Medicare.

To summarize this discussion of baseline computation, the conclusion regarding mandatory programs is the same as that for discretionary ones: the mechanical formulas used for current policy do not accurately reflect current services. Indeed, they are not intended to perform this task, despite the frequent labeling of current policy as current services. Estimating true current services would require an effort and form of analysis much more complex than those used to calculate current policy. And, in many cases, any measure of current services would be somewhat arbitrary.

How Current Policy Is Used

If current policy is not a useful proxy for current services, what then does current policy do? We shall see that the current policy baseline, designed to improve budget decisions, has resulted instead in a ritual of deficit "reduction" that frequently represents reduction only from the manipulated projections of the baseline, not in the actual deficit. We begin with how this baseline is used to maximize the amount of deficit reduction claimed, and then address four other uses of current policy.

The Maximization of Deficit Reduction

Americans and their politicians have usually supported balanced budgets, at least in principle. Before the 1980s, deficits were common but usually not large. Not large, at least, in comparison with the 1980s, when deficits reached peacetime records, $221 billion in 1986 and 6.3 percent of GNP in 1983.[29] As deficits climbed, Congress and the executive branch repeatedly claimed to be making massive reductions in the deficit. Although the need to reduce the deficit was usually framed against the goal of moving toward a balanced budget, which would require reducing the actual deficit, the deficit reductions trumpeted were instead measured against projections of the current policy baseline. For example, compared

TABLE 3.1
Proposed Budget Compromise

	FY 1988	FY 1989
Revenues		
Hard taxes	9.00	14.00
IRS compliance (net)	1.60	2.90
User fees	0.40	0.40
Subtotal	11.00	17.30
Spending		
Defense	5.00	8.20
Non-defense discretionary	2.60	3.40
1989 effect of 1988 2% pay	0.00	2.40
Entitlements		
Medicare	2.00	3.50
Farm price supports	0.90	1.60
GSL balances	0.25	0.00
Federal personnel	0.85	0.85
Subtotal, entitlements	4.00	5.95
Debt service	1.20	3.50
Subtotal, spending	12.80	23.45
Additional savings		
PBGC premiums	0.40	0.40
VA origination fee extension	0.20	0.20
VA loan guarantee	0.80	1.00
Asset sales	5.00	3.50
Subtotal	6.40	5.10
GRAND TOTAL	30.20	45.85

to the baseline projections of early 1981, it was claimed that spending cuts through January 1985 would reduce the projected deficit for 1986 by $63 billion, to a still-record level of $225 billion (as then projected). The reduction in national debt for the five-year period, calculated by adding claimed spending cuts for each year, was $239 billion.[30] During that time, the actual debt increased from $1.0 to $2.1 trillion.[31]

More recently, as Table 3.1 shows, the budget summit agreement of late 1987 claimed $30 billion in deficit reduction for 1988 and $46 billion for 1989. Although announced with great fanfare as a deficit-reduction plan, even after its implementation the deficit was projected to increase, not decrease. While the 1987 deficit was $150 billion, in January 1988 CBO projected a 1988 deficit of

$157 billion and a 1989 deficit of $176 billion.* But the goal of the summit was not to reduce the deficit below the level of 1987; the goal was instead to achieve sufficient reduction from current policy to avoid automatic cuts (called a sequester) under the Gramm-Rudman-Hollings Act.† Thus, during the budget negotiations, while working to implement the plan in Congress, and in discussions with the press, the negotiators never analyzed the plan's impact on year-to-year deficits, receipts, or spending.

Similarly, the budget summit of 1990 claimed large deficit reductions, while in fact the deficit reached record levels in fiscal 1991 and 1992. Spending estimates available at the time of the summit projected an increase in the deficit of 7.8 percent in 1991 and 2.3 percent in 1992.[32] Nevertheless, press coverage of the event focused almost exclusively on the claimed $500 billion deficit reduction. Table 3.2 shows the claimed deficit reduction of the legislation that actually passed, $496 billion. Unlike the 1987 summit agreement, however, the 1990 agreement was for five years, and the negotiators did project that the budget would be in balance or very close to it by the end of the time. This conclusion rested on very optimistic economic assumptions, however; perhaps for that reason, it was largely ignored in the press.[33]

Nowhere is the difference between the reality of yearly changes in a program and the arithmetic of the baseline greater than in Medicare. In 1980 expenditures for Medicare were $34 billion; the CBO baseline projection was $114 billion for 1991 and $173 billion for 1995. Under current growth rates, Medicare will surpass Defense and Social Security to become the single largest budget item early in the next century. Yet public discussion of Medicare typically focuses on how much the program is being "cut." Tables

*Under CBO projections made in the summer of 1987, the summit agreement seemed likely to reduce the actual deficit. But the negotiators knew that, following the stock market crash of October 1987, CBO would project a higher deficit path in January 1988.

†To the extent there was any consideration of 1989, and the author recalls only a few staff-level discussions, it reflected Congress's belief that OMB would, through optimistic economic and technical assumptions, make projections that avoided a sequester. During the negotiations, however, the administration did not present formal deficit projections for 1989. Preliminary estimates indicated that it would require considerable luck to avoid a sequester. Such good luck did occur: higher than projected economic growth reduced the deficit, as did the drought in the summer of 1988, which reduced farm subsidy payments.

TABLE 3.2
Estimated Budget Reductions: 1990 Budget Summit

	FY 1991	FY 1991–95
Revenues		
Taxes	17.6	137.2
IRS compliance	3.0	9.4
Spending		
Defense	10.0	182.4
Agriculture	1.5	14.2
Medicare	3.3	35.0
Federal personnel (including Postal Service)	2.3	14.5
Other	0.8	7.1
User fees and other offsetting receipts	2.5	28.1
Debt service	1.6	68.4
TOTAL	42.6	496.3

SOURCE: U.S. Senate, Budget Committee Majority, updated summary of the conference budget reconciliation bill (Oct. 30, 1990); Hoagland, "Omnibus Budget Reconciliation Act." (Mr. Hoagland is the Republican staff director of the Budget Committee). The staff majority's totals are used in the table; the minority's numbers are used only to fill in or check details unavailable or unclear from the majority report.

3.1 and 3.2 are illustrative. While a $5.5 billion "reduction" was listed for Medicare in the 1987 summit agreement, and as measured by CBO $5.9 billion was "cut," what this meant was *restraining the rate of increase* in the baseline between 1987 and 1989 from 25 to 20 percent.[34] Similarly, the $35 billion reduction claimed in the fall of 1990 merely restrained the rate of increase in the baseline between 1991 and 1995.[35]

Considering changes that actually were made explains why a program that has repeatedly been cut continues its rapid growth. $1.1 billion of the reduction achieved in the 1987 summit, or 19 percent, was achieved by moving some Medicare payments from the last few days of each fiscal year into the first few days of the next. The largest part of the remainder, $1.7 billion or 29 percent, was achieved by *restraining the increase* in the update for hospitals under the PPS system to below the full market-basket rate that figures in the CBO baseline. As explained above, Congress provided for a far higher update than in previous years, while still claiming this change as the largest single "reduction." At the 1990 summit, including the Part B premium provision as a Medicare "cut," $17.7 billion or 51 percent was "saved" although it simply extended provisions of current law, as will be explained below. Another $12.5 billion in savings, or 36 percent, was obtained through modest limits in the PPS update.

Our earlier discussion of medical spending showed how misleading the picture of Medicare "cuts" is. As noted, in early 1990, CBO estimated that from 1991 to 1995 the medical program's baseline would have increased by $179 billion because of increased use of medical services. The "cuts" actually obtained for the entire program were $35 billion ($43 billion, including the premium extension).* Thus, while an image of severe restraint was created, the spending projections did not keep pace with the incentives in the system for increasing use of medical services. As we will see below, even the small restraint achieved was undercut by subsequent changes in the estimates of projected medical spending.

The Vanishing Tax Increase

Under current services, projecting government revenue is straightforward: one calculates the total receipts that would be paid tomorrow under tax law as it exists today. Current policy is different. If taxes are enacted to be implemented five years hence, when the year of the increase arrives the new taxes do not count as increases—they are already "in the baseline." The 1987 budget summit provides an example. Although Table 3.1 shows modest (relative to total receipts) tax increases, which would only grow slightly beyond 1989, the reality is quite different. The following figures show the impact of the new receipts under the budget summit agreement through 1991, contrasted with the *total* new receipts to be collected after calendar 1987, including new taxes passed before 1987:[36]

	1988	1989	1990	1991
Budget summit new receipts	11.5	17.4	19.5	19.0
Total new receipts in laws implemented after 12/31/87	20.6	31.8	43.0	53.7

*The summit used a baseline slightly different from the one CBO had used in March 1990, when the $179 billion was calculated. No precise estimate of increased use is available for the baseline used in the fall of 1990.

The 1990 negotiations produced a different use of the phantom tax increase. Under current law, the telephone excise tax was set to expire. Congress and the Administration agreed to simply extend this tax, thus making it possible to claim increased revenues of $13.1 billion over five years.[37] These "new" revenues were used to fund a new child care program without, its proponents claimed, raising the deficit. The reality, however, is that taxes continued at the same level while spending in fact increased.

The Invisible Spending Increase

Spending increases are subject to the same sleight of hand: increases in programs not implemented until years after a bill's passage escape being counted as increases because, when the new spending actually occurs, it is "already in the baseline." The 1987 and 1990 budget summits illustrate this phenomenon. In the legislation that implemented the 1987 summit, Medicaid and income-support programs were expanded over five years by $3.6 billion, according to 1987 estimates of the Department of Health and Human Services (HHS).* These expansions were not prohibited by the budget summit agreement, in part because they did not significantly affect 1988 and 1989 spending; nor were offsetting reductions elsewhere required. In the 1990 budget negotiations, total estimated expansions over five years equaled $25.9 billion.† Moreover, one expansion of Medicaid expands coverage of certain children from age 6 to 18, with coverage to be extended by one year at a time. HHS estimates that this provision will cost $0.6 billion in 1995. Although precise estimates for the full cost when the age of covered children reaches 18 are unavailable, it will probably at least double.

Budget estimates for the expansion's initial years rarely reveal the potential size of such expansions. For example, two-thirds of the $3.6 billion in expansions enacted in 1987 occurred in 1991

*HHS usually estimates that program estimates will cost more than does CBO. I discuss below the estimation problems that have plagued both the legislative and executive branches regarding medical programs.

†This number uses CBO estimates and includes $12.1 billion for an expansion of the earned-income tax credit (see Hoagland 1990). The numbers in Table 3.2 count this expansion as an offset to a tax increase rather than an increase in spending.

and 1992. There are two reasons for such a pattern. First, program expansions take time to implement. Second, they are often written to delay full implementation for several years, precisely so that they can be included in the baseline and thus not show up as spending increases.

The experience of the budget summits is not unique. Many reconciliation bills have expanded Medicare and Medicaid. Based on HHS estimates, the 1987 Medicaid expansion would have added only $79 million to annual costs in 1988, but $1.2 billion by 1992. The expansions in the 1986 reconciliation bill cost $170 million for 1987, growing to nearly $500 million by 1992.* Indeed, between 1984 and 1988, there were 23 program changes in Medicaid, 22 of which mandated program expansions, as did each of the 20 provisions enacted after 1984, with the latter adding over $1 billion in annual program costs.[38]

The Perpetual Motion Machine of Expiring Spending Cuts

Under current policy a program is counted as "cut" if a policy designed to hold down costs is scheduled to expire and is then extended. This device has been used with increasing frequency to claim spending cuts. About $7 billion of the net $54 billion Medicare reductions claimed during the Reagan administration came through such extensions.[39] This practice was heavily used in the budget negotiations of 1990. As Table 3.3 shows, extending the policy that Medicare recipients pay 25 percent of the cost of Part B (for physicians' services) resulted in "cuts" of $7.5 billion;[40] capital payments to hospitals under Part A were continued at 85 percent of the maximum allowed, at least for 1991; and the law also extended the requirement that certain costs be borne by recipients' private insurance companies rather than Medicare. The capital provision is actually not an extension: whereas previously payments had been 85 percent of the maximum, payment for 1992 through 1995 will be 90 percent. Thus, savings of $4.1 billion were claimed even

*Using HHS estimates, the total Medicaid increase from these two reconciliation bills was $5.2 billion from 1988 to 1992, $1.7 billion of it in 1992. CBO estimates for the 1987 bill show a substantial increase in the later years, although of lesser magnitude.

TABLE 3.3
"Savings" in 1990 and 1991
from Extending Expired Provisions and Policies of Medicare
($ in billions)

	1991	1991–95
Hospital capital:		
extend 85% payment in 1991 only; increase payment to 90% in 1992–95	$0.8	$4.1
Part B premium: extend at 25%	0.0	7.5
Medicare secondary payer	.1	6.1
Total Medicare savings claimed	.9	17.7

though hospitals actually would receive more money than they would have under earlier provisions.[41]

Medicare is not the only area in which such devices have been used. The agriculture cuts shown in Table 3.1 were set to expire as well. Moreover, extending expiring taxes produced over $5 billion of the two-year receipt total shown in Table 3.1. Manipulation of pay increases has produced similar "savings." Beginning in 1984, pay raises took effect in January instead of the preceding October. The baseline, however, has often assumed that the pay raise would begin in October. Retention of the October assumption in the baseline produced three months of "savings" that could not otherwise have been claimed.

Discretionary Programs

Under current policy, defense has seen frequent changes. Until 1980, and since 1987, CBO simply inflated the previous year's level of expenditure, as it did other discretionary accounts. From 1981 to 1983, at the request of the Senate Budget Committee, CBO used a baseline resembling true current services, as discussed earlier. For the next three years, also at the request of the Senate committee, the baseline changed again, this time to equal the amounts allocated to the out-years in previous Congressional budget resolutions.

The Reagan administration supported high defense baselines because they made it easier to increase defense spending.* Because

*Indeed, as noted earlier, the administration greatly inflated its defense baseline, using a baseline of "adequate defense" for 1982, which equated the baseline and presidential policy.

Congress did not appropriate all that the administration wanted, the inflated baselines allowed Congress to claim very large budget savings, particularly in 1986. The 1985 appropriation was $295 billion, while the baseline for 1986 was $325 billion, allowing Congress to claim that its provision of $303 billion for 1986 represented $22 billion in deficit reduction, though in fact it was an $8 billion increase above the previous year's appropriation.

Tables 3.1 and 3.2 use the current practice for both defense and nondefense discretionary accounts, inflating the previous year's level. Thus, the $19.2 billion in savings for defense and nondefense in Table 3.1 over two years represented an approximate average of 2 percent in annual growth from 1987 levels.

As Table 3.2 shows, the negotiators claimed $182.4 billion in discretionary savings over five years. All these "savings" resulted from projected defense spending below the inflation-adjusted baseline.* Thus, defense provided almost 40 percent of the claimed deficit reduction. Although the United States will undoubtedly spend less on defense in the 1990s, adjusted for inflation, than in the 1980s, this change will not be the result of the budget summit of 1990, but of the decline in the Soviet threat. Nevertheless, in taking credit for the certain moderation in defense spending, both Congress and the executive significantly inflated their claimed savings from the 1990 negotiations.

Another problem with the defense baseline emerged when CBO switched its defense baseline for 1987. New budget authority produces outlays at different rates. Programs that fund people and operations and maintenance, for example, tend to start producing outlays quickly; by contrast, procurement programs, such as those for building ships, begin producing outlays slowly. CBO's formula for the current policy baseline simply inflated the budget authority for the previous year, holding constant whatever mix between fast and slow spending programs had previously existed. This me-

*Technically, the 1990 summit agreed only on defense reductions for 1991–93, with additional savings to be taken from the combined discretionary accounts, including both domestic and international programs. In reality, however, the negotiators could not agree on defense levels beyond 1993, with the congressional Democrats favoring reductions greater than the administration and greater than implied by the $182.4 billion figure. Even if they had promised to stipulate in writing the defense levels implied by the $182.4 billion number, the Democrats would have been unwilling to guarantee the amount for 1994–95. The negotiators understood that defense spending would decrease by *at least* $182.4 billion.

chanical calculation produced a "mismatch" between the outlay estimate of the baseline and the outlays that would occur under any program mix Congress was likely to approve.* As Congress stopped the large increases of the first Reagan term and as plans for massive new procurement subsided, Congress allocated an increasing percentage of new money to faster spending programs. The baseline, retaining the mix between faster and slower spending in the previous year's budget, allocated too much to slower-spending programs and accordingly did not produce enough outlays for the congressionally mandated program. With the administration's support, Congress used sleight of hand to solve the problem. In 1987, for example, Congress simply shifted the final pay date from the last day of 1987 to the first day of 1988, "saving" about $3 billion.

This change in dates was not the only use of pay policy to produce large paper savings. For example, the three-year savings claimed in the 1983 first budget resolution were $9.3 billion, although federal employees received a pay increase of 4 percent, increasing outlays for pay over the three years by $5.8 billion.[42] Overall, the CBO baseline for pay increases between 1983 and 1988 exceeded 4 percent, while pay increased less than 3 percent, with an average spread between the baseline and actual increase of about 1.5 percent—which were counted as "savings."

Table 3.1 provides a recent example of claimed pay "cuts," $2.4 billion for 1989. Following past practice, savings for 1988 would have been claimed as well. But because of a technicality in the Gramm-Rudman-Hollings law, the baseline in effect for 1988 when the budget summit began used the same figure as the actual planned pay increase, 2 percent. Accordingly, there could be no reduction claimed for 1988. But Gramm-Rudman-Hollings did not apply to 1989 calculations. Because the 1989 baseline assumed a 1988 increase of about 4 percent, paying a 2 percent increase in 1988 would produce paper savings in 1989, even if pay increased by 4 percent or more in 1989.

Yet the Appropriations Committees received, under the agreement, fixed amounts that could be used for any item, including

*CBO noted the mismatch in its 1988 baseline report, issued in January 1987, p. 58. But because correcting the problem required moving away from a mechanical calculation, it was reluctant to change.

pay increases. If told they must appropriate less money for pay increases, they would simply have more money to appropriate for other purposes. Trimming pay reduces the deficit only if the *total* available appropriation is lowered accordingly. The summit agreement of 1987 did not lower the overall appropriation. Thus, whether or not a 2 percent pay increase is really a pay cut, because $2.4 billion was not taken from the Appropriations Committees for 1989, the deficit was not reduced.*

Keeping Score

Thus far, we have discussed *projections* of savings from the current policy baseline. We have not considered whether savings actually occur, even as measured from current policy. At least three problems immediately present themselves in attempting such a calculation. One involves the vagaries of estimation, as unexpected events may increase or decrease actual spending or receipts. Another involves manipulation of the baseline to produce paper savings that do not occur even from the baseline figure. Finally, there is the "hold harmless" practice, by which increased funds are allowed for certain programs without being counted as increases.

The vagaries of estimation are well-known problems in certain areas of the budget. Budget estimates released early in calendar 1991 provide a recent example, and one of the most dramatic. For the five years covered by the 1990 Budget Summit, re-estimates of baseline spending increased for Medicaid and Medicare by $49 billion, significantly higher than the alleged severe "cuts" of $35.6 billion in the Medicare and Medicaid baseline during the 1990 budget summit. Thus, compared to projections of six months earlier, Medicaid and Medicare are projected to spend billions more, even after the budget summit "cuts." The reasons for the re-estimates

*Majority staff from the Senate Budget Committee dispute this argument. They claim that the calculation used to obtain the 1989 number did remove funding for increases from the appropriators. But the claimed discretionary savings for 1989 in Table 3.1 simply reflects having 2 percent more in 1989 than in 1988 instead of the higher percentage for inflation assumed in the baseline. To add the $2.4 billion not spent for pay increases as additional reduction increases the nominal savings without actually restricting the ability of the appropriators to spend money. In any event, the general point remains. Claimed pay savings will not reduce the deficit unless the money is actually taken from the appropriators; merely passing a pay raise lower than the baseline assumption does not accomplish this.

vary, but the "restraint" in 1990 and previous years is trivial compared to the total program and its rapidly increasing projections.

Another example involves agriculture. Between 1972 and 1986, the Department of Agriculture's yearly estimates of outlays for its commodity programs, totaling $63.8 billion, were $46.9 billion below actual spending.[43] On the other hand, estimates from the U.S. Postal Service of the additional funding it would require between 1980 and 1985 exceeded the amount actually needed by an annual average of $1.1 billion.[44]

Just as estimators can have difficulty calculating overall program levels, so can they have difficulty estimating the impact of changes from the baseline. Expenditures under Medicare Part B, dealing with payments to physicians, are illustrative. During the 1983 budget deliberations, physician current policy outlays were projected to double from 1982 to 1987, even though inflation over the period was projected to be only 27 percent.[45] From 1983 to 1987, numerous "cuts" were enacted. CBO's estimates of savings at the time of enactment were $6.5 billion from the current policy baseline, $2.4 billion in 1987 alone. Although inflation over the period was less than expected—16, not 27, percent—and $6.5 billion had been "cut," physician spending for 1987 was actually $800 million more than the projection at the beginning of fiscal 1982. Thus, despite the large amount of claimed savings and despite inflation only about 60 percent as high as projected, *actual* spending was higher than the baseline assumed.[46]

Other Medicare savings have also been overestimated. For example, the Deficit Reduction Act of 1984 replaced a fee-for-service reimbursement system for clinical labs with a fee schedule, with saving estimated at $1 billion over four years. The savings have not materialized because the fee schedule was set too high, resulting merely in a redistribution of payments among providers.[47]

The impact of many expansions has been underestimated as well. Again, Medicare, where so much of the claimed deficit reduction has occurred, provides examples. The Social Security Amendments of 1972 extended Medicare coverage to all victims of end-stage renal disease. In 1974, payments were $200 million for 16,000 patients; by 1986, there were 90,000 patients and annual costs of $2 billion, numbers much higher than originally estimated. Moreover, in 1986 Congress expanded the number of providers who can offer vision-care services, estimating the cost to be $160 million over the first three years. Actual experience revealed a cost per year of nearly $200 million.[48]

Besides the technical estimation problem, there is the second problem—pure gimmickry. Many savings are claimed from the baseline that, even accepting the baseline methodology, do not reduce the deficit. One frequent example is pushing outlays into the year preceding or the year following the budget year. The military pay shift discussed above is illustrative. Agricultural outlays have frequently been manipulated in this manner as well. Moreover, $1.1 billion of the $5.9 billion reduction for Medicare claimed in the budget summit of 1987 was such a shift, achieved by paying hospitals a few days more slowly. Further, $1.4 billion of the claimed additional receipts in Table 3.1 represented speeding up collections of taxes. And about $400 million of the personnel savings for 1989 in Table 3.1 were obtained by placing funds in escrow until 1990.

Manipulation of the appropriations process is also frequent. Savings that require reductions in appropriations are sometimes counted but the reductions are not actually made, as the 1989 pay number in Table 3.1 reveals. Other examples involve reductions made in authorization bills, without corresponding reductions in actual appropriations.[49]

A final type of scoring problem arose during the 1990 budget negotiations. In all three areas of discretionary spending (defense, domestic, international), the claimed reductions are "held harmless" from certain spending programs. For example, defense reductions do not allow for any increases incurred by Desert Shield and Desert Storm, domestic discretionary spending was given extra funds as a "sweetner" to clinch the budget deal, and future spending for emergencies did not need to be offset. These hold-harmless provisions are agreements to simply ignore the impact of events. Accordingly, the final result of the budget deal will be tens of billions of dollars in outlays not counted in the $496 billion number in Table 3.2.

A further variant of the hold-harmless concept involves the Earned Income Tax Credit (EITC). The 1990 legislation dramatically extended this provision, which eliminates the taxes owed by many of the working poor. Indeed, in most cases the credit exceeds the tax liabilities, resulting in a government outlay, not just a cut in taxes. The traditional way this program is scored counted the amount in excess of tax liability as an outlay.[50] The 1990 negotiators desired both to reduce the total tax increases claimed in the agreement and to hold the claimed entitlement savings harmless from the impact of the EITC. Accordingly, they netted the EITC against the planned tax increases, not against entitlement reductions. Thus, the proper amount of tax increases, using the conventional EITC scoring before 1990, was actually $149.2 billion, rather than $137.2 billion. Entitlement savings were $58.8 billion, not $70.8 billion as claimed in Table 3.2.[51]

Agriculture provides yet another version of this approach. The Reconciliation Act passed in 1990 provides for a reduction in the announced reductions in commodity price support should a GATT agreement not be entered into by the United States by June 30, 1992. Further, if no GATT agreement is in force by June 30, 1993, the Secretary of Agriculture may waive all or part of the reductions claimed in the Reconciliation Act. These detriggering provisions could reduce the savings in Table 3.2 by over $5 billion.[52]

The Impact of the Current Policy Baseline

Responding to polls showing public concern, politicians stress the need to reduce the deficit. Although such reduction literally means reducing the deficit below the actual level of the previous year's deficit, the political goal has instead become to "cut" from the current policy baseline, and then proclaim the resulting number as satisfying the public's desire. Current policy has thus replaced last year's level as the base most frequently used to measure budget proposals. Although programs and the deficit are claimed to be "cut," that word has a different meaning in Washington than elsewhere.* Using the current policy baseline, programs can still spend

*The reaction of the nongovernment members of the National Economic Commission, created to propose solutions to ever-increasing deficits, is noteworthy. When the current policy baseline was explained, many expressed surprise, consternation, or both. "I didn't know that," exclaimed Robert Strauss when told that ever-increasing program levels would not be called an increase if built into current law. "If we did this in business, they'd lock us up," said Lee Iacocca. NEC 1988 (reaction to the author's testimony on baselines).

more than in the previous year yet count as cuts; under a system using the previous year's expenditure as the base, increases would be called just that, increases.[53]

Proponents of the baseline approach both argue its necessity and maintain that "objections [to the baseline system] have more to do with form than substance. . . . In the end, the budget totals are the same whichever approach is used."[54] Yet any system that fundamentally alters how the public understands political action influences outcomes. Indeed, this pattern continued in the budget negotiations of 1990. The rhetoric that dominated the process was of extreme pain, yet Congress expanded Medicare and Medicaid significantly and continued the large increases in domestic discretionary spending that began in the last year of the Reagan administration. The reality of substantial new spending hardly matched the harsh rhetoric of severe restraint.

The rhetoric of the budget is biased toward increased spending. This claim can be reduced to a simple proposition: In dealing with the press and public, would an advocate for a program prefer that built-in increases above the previous year's levels be characterized as "current," so that a restraint in growth leaving expenditures well above last year's would be presented as a "cut"? Or, would he prefer to have the debate be over the 12 percent increase assumed in the baseline, or a mere 9 percent increase over last year's spending levels? Particularly given the short time one often has to make one's point—in many cases a 20–30 second "sound byte"—it would be a rare program advocate indeed who did not prefer the current policy language of "cut" to the alternative of defending an annual increase.

The defenders of the current Medicare and Medicaid programs provide an excellent example. On January 5, 1987, the President's budget for 1988 was released, which proposed to restrain the growth in Medicare from 63 percent (10 percent annually) in the administration's current policy baseline for 1987 to 1991 to 46 percent (8 percent annually) and to restrain the growth rate in all medical programs from 9 percent to 6 percent. The next day, the American Association of Retired Persons, the American Hospital Association, the American Medical Association, the American Nurses Association, and the Federation of American Health

Systems ran a full-page advertisement carried in the *Washington Post*.

The ad featured a large picture of an elderly woman and a young soldier embracing. The following appeared above the picture:

> During the past 5 years,
> more than $30 billion has been
> cut from Medicare and Medicaid.
> Now the Administration
> wants to cut $50 billion more.

Below the picture, the ad asked:

> Isn't it time we started
> defending the home front?

The body of the ad appears to compare yearly increases in defense spending with "cuts" in medical programs. Against the current policy baseline, Medicare and Medicaid had indeed been cut. Yet, in absolute numbers, national defense outlays grew by 110 percent from 1980 to 1987 ($134 billion to $282 billion), while Medicare and Medicaid increased by 119 percent ($47 billion to $103 billion). Thus, the medical programs actually grew by a *greater* percentage than defense. By claiming that defense was increasing while Medicare and Medicaid were being cut, however, the ad effectively used the current policy baseline to protect double-digit growth in the medical programs.*

The manipulation of the baseline exacerbates this bias in favor of spending. When, as in the 1990 budget summit, $17 billion can be claimed as "cuts" simply by extending current law (and even paying hospitals a higher percentage for capital than previously), when $9 billion can be claimed as savings over three years by limiting pay increases to 4 percent, when paying hospitals a higher update than they previously received is the largest "cut" in the 1987 budget summit category of entitlement "savings," and when money can simply be shifted to the next fiscal year to claim savings, a large

*After testifying before the NEC, I received only one call from a health care lobbyist. To my surprise, he was not upset at the concern the nongovernmental members expressed about the current policy baseline, but instead wanted to know the basis for my calculation that Medicare has been "cut" by more than the lobbyist had thought. He wanted to use the higher number in upcoming congressional testimony.

TABLE 3.4
Reagan-Era Medicare Reductions from Current Policy Baseline Projections
($ in billions)

Hospital payments	$17
Extending current law	7
Physician savings	12
Hard savings	17
Soft savings	6
Expansions	−5
Net savings	54

package of "reductions" can be enacted with little or no impact on actual spending or the deficit. The goal of the budget process has become producing a respectable number of "cuts"; if the cuts merely manipulate the baseline, the political pain, which is greater when programs are actually cut than when they are increased, is lessened.[55] More important, some of these "cuts" are then used to offset real spending increases or to protect other programs from real spending restraint. Congress frequently pays for new initiatives, which can dramatically increase outlays, by "cuts" from the baseline. In this way "soft" savings offset "hard" increases.

Manipulation of the baseline probably reaches its peak with respect to Medicare. The dollar outlay for Medicare tripled during the 1980s, yet taking the estimates of CBO made at or near the time of enactment, $54 billion in "cuts" occurred.[56] Table 3.4 breaks this $54 billion into six categories.

The bulk of the hospital "savings" result from a law passed in 1983 to restrict the rate of growth in spending. Ironically, the hospital savings do not include the most significant success in restraining spending, namely the introduction of the Prospective Payment System (PPS).* In their first year under PPS, participating hospitals reduced the rate of growth in their costs by more than half compared with hospitals still operating under the previous system.[57] Nevertheless, the impact of the PPS system is itself ironic. Before this system was instituted, the current policy baseline for operating margins was zero, but in 1984 and 1985 the average operating

*The hospital payments category does not include all hospital savings, but only those that do not fit in the other categories.

margins on Medicare business were 15 percent. Thus, despite the "cut," hospital profits increased. No doubt, Medicare saved money under PPS, but had the increase in margins been avoided or at least minimized, costs would have been reduced still more.* An additional problem with PPS has been the use of the market basket as the baseline. Large savings have been claimed, although annual updates have exceeded past levels and margins for many hospitals exceeded pre-PPS levels.

Extension of current law, whereby expiring provisions can be repeatedly claimed for deficit reduction, is a category representing simple manipulation of the baseline. The physicians' "savings" were estimates projected to result from changes in physician incentives, which in fact never materialized. Indeed, as discussed above, actual spending on doctors has *exceeded* the estimates of the baseline made *before* the "cuts" were enacted.

The soft savings shown in Table 3.4 involve estimates that were particularly speculative or that never occurred, as in the clinical lab example given earlier. Hard savings involve actual reductions from current policy. The expansions are for Medicare only, and do not include the few billion dollars in Medicaid expansions that have normally been "paid for" through reductions from the Medicare baseline. Nor do they include expansions in other programs that have been paid for in the same way. Most important, they also exclude the expansionary impact of the enacted bills compared to the administration's proposals for more restrictive regulations. In part because the baseline is rising far faster than inflation plus the increase in numbers of patients, Congress and the executive have tried to restrain Medicare's growth. As we have seen, the problem is that providers and patients respond to the incentives in the current system—incentives that cause medical inflation to exceed general inflation. With the notable exception of PPS, which itself produced less real restraint than it could have had windfall profits been avoided, a large amount of the claimed deficit reduction has been nothing more than a mostly failed effort to change these incentives. The reestimate of increased medical spending that exceeded the 1990 summit's claimed reductions is but the latest manifestation of failure.

*Of course, some increase in margins may have provided a useful incentive to exert greater cost control, even for so-called nonprofit hospitals. The actual increase, however, greatly exceeded any amount intended for that purpose.

Yet the rhetoric of "cuts" has come to dominate discussions of Medicare. The author has heard many members of Congress—even those on the appropriations committees, who are most likely to gain from real restraint—state that Medicare has been cut so much that there is little left to reduce. Thus, despite the explosive growth in the program, few changes were made at the 1990 summit. Simply extending current law (and even paying hospitals more for capital than they previously received) and manipulating the annual PPS update to hospitals produced $26.5 billion, or 62 percent of the total claimed Medicare reductions.[58] It is hard to escape the conclusion that the baseline system has served proponents of increased Medicare spending.

The budget process has wandered far from the original purposes of Senator Muskie and the others who instituted the baseline system. A device created to promote good government has become instead an exercise in gamesmanship to justify politically expedient results. If one is schooled in the economics of politics, it is not surprising that a system has been developed, with accompanying rhetoric and rules, that is biased toward increased spending.[59] From this viewpoint, politicians will attempt to manipulate any budget system. Nevertheless, the present-day use of the current policy baseline represents the Sistine Chapel of that art.

Even for conservative politicians who truly want to emphasize deficit reduction, the baseline system maximizes the deficit reduction that can be claimed. Indeed, at the key point in the history of the use of baselines, 1981, it was easy to see the emergence of a mutually beneficial, political "bargain" to use current policy as the baseline in budget negotiations. Although Republicans on the Senate Budget Committee had ridiculed current policy in the late 1970s, they acquiesced in the administration's use of it in 1981, which magnified the apparent size of the savings. Liberals were appeased because the actual reductions were lower than they appeared to be. As Allen Schick has said, "Republicans claimed more savings and the Democrats saved more programs, a happy combination for political institutions faced with difficult choices."*

The effect of the baseline can also be seen in press accounts of the budget. Consider, for example, a *New York Times* front-page

*Schick 1982, p. 32. Use of current policy also assisted the Administration's efforts to appease the business community, which feared that large tax cuts would not be offset by spending cuts. Moreover, the use of the baseline, by maximizing the

story on President Reagan's fiscal 1987 budget headlined "Reagan's Budget Asking Cutbacks in Health Plans, Increases in Military."[60] The *Washington Post*'s lead story on that budget claimed that the President was proposing "about $23 billion in domestic program cuts for next year while adding $33 billion for National Defense."[61] Other accounts were similar.[62] These stories compare an increase in the defense budget above the previous year's with reductions from the current policy baseline for other programs. Budget concepts have thus caused confusion and, as with the Medicare-Medicaid advertisement cited above, have conveyed the impression that "cuts" are being made from the actual spending levels of the year before.

Polling data and their uses also show the confusion caused by the current policy baseline. For example, polls show that Americans oppose reducing Medicare. This fact is widely repeated as a rejection of future "cuts" in Medicare.[63] Indeed, almost all Americans say they want funding to increase for medical programs. But because these polls simply ask whether spending should increase or decrease, they tell us nothing *per se* about support for changes from the current policy projections. Because the baseline now has Medicare spending increasing at over 10 percent annually, only by asking whether that percentage is appropriate can polling reveal how Americans feel.

Conclusion

Created to give policymakers a better handle on budgetary decisions, in practice the current policy baseline has given rise to a charade divorced from fiscal realities. It should be scrapped.

The baseline system has proved to have serious flaws. First, although current policy is often called current services, it does not

---

amount of cuts claimed, helped give the impression that the overall package, which required some politically painful votes, was worth the effort. In its revision of the last Reagan budget, the Bush administration attacked the baseline system, calling it a "wonderland phenomenon" (see Presidential Documents, p. 23). Within a few months, however, the administration returned to use of the current policy baseline. The administration's February approach to the budget was criticized, although much of the criticism was not for its use of the previous year as the base, but for its failure to reveal account-level detail for its proposals.

measure those services in practice. The technicians who prepare the baseline, particularly in CBO, must, because of institutional concerns, rely on formulas often inconsistent with current services. Even if those formulas were abandoned, the results would frequently be subject to reasonable dispute at best and to arbitrary manipulation at worst.

Second and more important, current policy is misused in portraying whether spending, receipts, and the deficit are actually increasing or decreasing. By raising the cost of understanding the budget, the current policy baseline reduces the capacity of voters to make informed electoral choices. The public, and indeed most of those in Washington unskilled in the technicalities of the current policy baseline, understand the deficit and spending totals as absolute numbers. Calls for reduction mean reductions below previous years' levels. This simple understanding should be the guiding principle. Programs should be discussed on a year-to-year basis, not in terms of a hypothetical baseline. The debate should be over the *level* of receipts, outlays, and deficits under various alternatives, not over the magnitude of manipulated "cuts" from inflated projections.

Of course, the problems that led to the baseline system cannot be ignored. As now calculated, the current policy baseline does provide useful information for many programs, i.e., a knowledge of what spending would be in the absence of congressional action. But for many other programs, notably discretionary programs, and those parts of mandatory programs that require frequent adjustments, there is no automatic pilot to measure. Rather than pretend to solve an insoluble problem, we should acknowledge that no good baseline is possible.

Although all programs should be measured against the base of the previous year's spending, for those programs that automatically increase the underlying reasons should be understood and evaluated. Breaking down the increases in programs into their components would improve Congressional and public understanding of the dynamics of government spending. For Medicare, for example, the past year's spending could be presented along with the projected increase in beneficiaries, changes caused by the aging of the population, general inflation, medical inflation, increased volume and intensity of use, and the costs of phasing in expansions and expiring provisions. To be sure, such a procedure would be more complex than using current policy baseline alone, but it would be a more accurate picture of reality. Medicare and many other government programs are not simple. Understanding and making intelligent decisions about those programs requires knowing why and how the program is growing. If the presentation of these programs oversimplifies a complex reality, it conceals important information and indirectly influences outcomes. The technical display should be as neutral as possible.

One of the major justifications that proponents of the current policy baseline give for inflating discretionary programs is that estimates are made for five years. Freezing such programs for that long, they claim, is unrealistic. For many programs, they are no doubt right. In evaluating the level of spending on discretionary programs over five years, or over eight as is done in the next chapter, there is considerable justification for wanting to know not only the nominal dollar totals, but also constant dollar totals—i.e., totals adjusted for the impact of inflation. For the annual appropriations process, however, except in years of rampant inflation, this point is irrelevant. Decisions are usually made one year at a time, not for five or eight years.

Of course last year's level may provide inadequate funding for the goals desired, including maintaining the previous level of services. For example, a pay freeze may have adverse effects on attracting and keeping quality employees. But it is needlessly confusing to characterize a pay increase above last year's level, but below the current policy baseline, as a cut. Using last year as the base still permits debate over the adequacy of the pay increase, but it avoids confusion over the impact a pay increase will have on the deficit.

No system of evaluating budget decisions will be entirely immune from distortion and gamesmanship. But abandoning the current policy baseline system will make it easier to understand the impact of spending and tax decisions on the deficit. And it will decrease the ability of those in Washington to claim victories in numerous battles against the deficit while steadily losing the war.

4

Changes in Discretionary Domestic Spending During the Reagan Years

JOHN F. COGAN and TIMOTHY J. MURIS

Introduction

A commonly held view about the federal budget is that discretionary domestic spending was cut drastically during the 1980s. This belief is perhaps best summarized by William Gray's colorful statement that "we've squeezed the fat, the skin and some of the muscle out of these domestic programs. Now we're down to the marrow." According to this view, the other two major parts of government spending, entitlements and defense, increased, leaving the domestic discretionary category to bear the brunt of the efforts to control government spending. By the latter part of the 1980s, this view became a virtual ritualistic incantation in budget hearings, newspapers, statements by congressional leaders, and comments by observers of the budget process.[1]

The incantation often contains a second part. The allegations of severe cuts are frequently followed by comments that these cuts have unduly restrained spending on key programs in the discretionary spending category such as education, public infrastructure, housing and nutrition for the poor, research and development.[2]

This chapter examines the actual record of government aggregate nonentitlement (discretionary) domestic spending. Contrary to popular belief, we find that domestic discretionary spending was not severely restrained in the 1980s.[3] Our analysis demonstrates that overall domestic discretionary spending grew only slightly less than the economy-wide inflation rate. Between 1981 and 1989, domestic discretionary spending increased by 32 percent, while inflation raised the price level by 35 percent. Hence, contrary to conventional wisdom, the 1980s was not a decade of severe cuts in domestic programs. Although there were deep budget reductions in the first full budget year of the Reagan administration, substantial budget growth occurred in most years thereafter. By the end of the decade, the growth had virtually restored the first year's cuts, and total domestic spending was almost equal to its 1981 inflation-adjusted level.

In addition, many individual programs whose budgets have purportedly been cut or severely restrained over this period received substantial increases. For example, even after adjusting for inflation, education programs for the handicapped increased by 50 percent; biomedical science research sponsored by the National Institutes of Health increased by 47 percent; the basic science research sponsored by the National Science Foundation grew by 38 percent; the Federal Aviation Administration's programs for safety and general operations increased by 36 percent; funding for the federal prison system rose by more than 200 percent; and the Women, Infants, and Children's program that provides nutritional assistance to pregnant women and newborn children rose by 54 percent. Indeed, the budgets of each of these programs grew faster than defense during President Reagan's years in office.

The restraint that did occur in domestic spending was concentrated in relatively few programs. Large program reductions in eight areas—the Comprehensive Employment and Training Program (CETA), Energy, Community Planning and Development, Mass Transit, Postal Service subsidies for special classes of mailers, Rails subsidies, Corps of Engineers Water Projects, and family support administrative services—account for most of the domestic budget cutting. The $26 billion in constant dollars that was cut from the programs of these bureaus between 1981 and 1989 accounts for about three-fourths of all bureau-level budget cuts in domestic discretionary spending. Placed in the context of total domestic discretionary spending, these cuts can be viewed as having financed a 19 percent constant-dollar growth in the remaining portion of the domestic budget.

The conventional wisdom about nonentitlement domestic

spending in the 1980s is based partly on anecdotal evidence and partly on the misuse of officially reported budget authority and outlays figures. Neither budget authority nor outlays necessarily measures the monetary size of programs accurately. The availability of means of financing programs other than direct appropriations, such as receipts from user fees, transfers from entitlement programs, and limitations on obligations, can increase program size without affecting budget authority and outlays. Also, for some programs with peculiar accounting conventions, such as housing and loan programs, budget authority and outlays bear no necessary conceptual relation to program size. For these programs, appropriations can be (and were) cut without affecting program size.

To properly gauge the monetary size of programs, we develop a new measure, *budgetary resources*. Budgetary resources for a program are the total amount of funds made available for obligation by that program in a given year. This measure includes all available means of financing. Once this measure is developed, a true picture of changes in domestic discretionary spending can be seen.

To explain these conclusions in more detail, the first section discusses how program size should be measured. The second section defines domestic discretionary spending and explains why subsidized housing and credit programs are not comparable with other domestic programs. The third section then presents empirical results based on the measurement techniques previously discussed. The final section contains concluding remarks.

How to Measure Program Size

The commonly held view that domestic discretionary spending was "pared to the bone" during the 1980s probably had its origin in the extraordinary success of the Reagan administration in accomplishing its agenda during its first year in office. On the spending side of the budget ledger, the 1981 Omnibus Budget Reconciliation Act reduced authorized levels for numerous domestic programs, and reductions contained in the ensuing domestic appropriation bills were historic in magnitude.[4] Press reports of these actions were widespread and helped shape the prevailing view. First impressions can be lasting, and it appears that this initial year was extrapolated to future years.

Moreover, annual reports of the Congressional Budget Office

(CBO) provide a historical data series on federal outlays by various program categories. Outlays for domestic discretionary programs according to this series show a more than 20 percent constant-dollar decline between 1981 and 1989.[5] Outlays, however, are not necessarily an accurate measure of the monetary size of government programs. The most serious deficiency of outlays is that they are recorded net of certain payments made to the government, called offsetting receipts or collections. Many of these are received from the public for businesslike activities such as the sale of services or products.[6] Others are received as transfers from entitlement domestic programs, defense, or international programs. A proper measure of program size must include the resources made available as the result of these receipts or transfers.

A second deficiency of outlays for measuring the monetary size of programs is that they occur at the end of the governmental funding process; they are recorded when obligations of the government are paid. Thus, outlays during any fiscal year pay for some obligations incurred in prior years and some incurred in the same year. Indeed, in a typical year during the 1980s, only about 60 percent of all outlays resulted from congressional appropriation decisions in that year.

If outlays are not an accurate monetary measure of program size, what measure is appropriate? What should be measured is the total amount of additional spending authority provided to governmental agencies to operate a program each year. Understanding why this measure is appropriate requires understanding how the government funding process operates. Government agencies are granted authority under statute to incur obligations. New authority to incur obligations granted by law constitutes the new *budgetary resources* available to an agency each year. The most common form of budgetary resources is budget authority provided through annual appropriations. For most discretionary programs, appropriated budget authority is by far the major source of budgetary resources.[7]

Can we then simply aggregate budget authority to measure program size? Unfortunately, this simple method would provide an incomplete measure. Many programs have sources of budgetary resources that are not reflected in or accurately measured by appropriated budget authority. For example, the appropriations committees use obligation limitations to control certain programs with trust funds or revolving funds. Highway programs, for example, are financed through a trust fund that receives money each year, primarily from taxes earmarked for this purpose. A limit on the amount in the fund that can be obligated, called an obligation limitation, controls the amount that can be obligated each year.[8] For these programs, obligation limitations serve the same purpose as an appropriation in other accounts. Thus, obligation limitations should be equated with appropriated budget authority in determining the amount of budgetary resources available to programs with such limitations.[9]

In other programs, Congress determines the amount annually available through a limitation on administrative expenses, not through an annual appropriation of budget authority. For example, benefit payments in programs such as Social Security and unemployment insurance are entitlements, which are not controlled through the appropriations process. The appropriations committees, however, establish annual limitations on the amount of these funds that can be used to administer such entitlements; that is, these administrative funds are discretionary. For example, the appropriation bill for the Departments of Labor, Health and Human Services, and Education each year sets the amounts from the Social Security Act trust funds that can be used for administrative expenses. Like obligation limitations, these amounts are identical to budget authority in providing the authority to make obligations, but they are excluded from reported totals of budget authority.

There are still other sources of budgetary resources. Domestic programs can be financed by proprietary receipts from the public; transfers from entitlement, other nondiscretionary domestic programs, and defense or international programs; and recoveries of prior-year obligations. Table 4.1, providing the actual budget data for the Patent and Trademark Office, helps explain how one of these other means of financing is accounted for in the budget process.

In this program, reported budget authority and outlays show no increase during the 1980s.[10] The actual amount made available for obligation (i.e., the budgetary resources), however, almost doubled. Receipts from the public explain the difference.

During the 1980s, Congress shifted part of the office's financing

TABLE 4.1
Means of Financing: Patient and Trademark Office
($ in millions)

	1981	1989
Budget authority	$116	$109
Proprietary receipts	0	112
Total, budgetary resources	116	201
Outlays	112	108

SOURCE: U.S. OMB, *Budget* (Appendix), FY 1983 and 1991.

from regular appropriations to revenues collected from patent and trademark application fees. During the last days of the Carter administration, Congress specified that fixed percentages (ranging from 25 to 100 percent) of the various bureau activities be financed through user fees.[11] The law provided that, starting in fiscal 1983, application fees were to be applied to offset appropriations instead of being deposited in the general fund. Two years later, at the Reagan administration's request, Congress raised application fees and required that revenues derived from these fees be available to the agency in lieu of budget authority to finance its operations.[12] Because the funds received from the fees charged are available to incur obligations, they must be added to budget authority to obtain an accurate monetary measure of program size. Thus, in nominal dollars the program has actually *increased* dramatically, not slightly decreased, as the budget authority and outlay numbers imply.[13]

The use of earmarked receipts from the public to increase the actual size of programs without a comparable increase in recorded budget authority and outlays became common in recent years.[14] Consider antitrust enforcement, which is split between the Department of Justice and the Federal Trade Commission. In fiscal 1989, the two agencies received an appropriation totaling $111.2 million.[15] The appropriation for 1990 provided $85.7 million in budget authority, an apparent decrease of 22.9 percent. But the appropriators intended to make $126.6 million available for the year, an increase of 13.9 percent, because businesses would now pay the government a fee when they filed proposed mergers with the agencies. (Before businesses can consummate many mergers, they are

TABLE 4.2

Means of Financing: Agriculture Stabilization and Conservation Service Administrative Expenses

($ in millions)

	1981	1989
Budget authority	$209	$0
Transfers (primarily from CCC)	157	619
User fees	2	43
Total: Budgetary resources	368	662
Outlays	183	−14

SOURCE: U.S. OMB, *Budget* (Appendix) FY 1983 and 1991. (The total transfer for FY 1989 includes a $381 thousand transfer from departmental administration for rental payments on a building to the General Services Administration.)

required to file information about them with the antitrust agencies and to wait a specific period during which the agencies decide whether to oppose the merger in federal court.)

Another means of financing program spending, transfers, is used for the salaries and expenses of the Department of Agriculture's Stabilization and Conservation Service (ASCS). The ASCS administers the farm price-support, conservation, and supply adjustment programs of the department. The administrative structure is large and complex, with federal expenditures totaling $660 million in 1989. These expenditures are primarily for the costs of more than 2,000 federal employees and nearly 16,000 nonfederal employees who are part of the farmer committee system.[16]

This administrative structure is financed through direct appropriation of budget authority, transfers from the Commodity Credit Corporation, and user fees collected from farmers for various services. During the 1980s, the method of financing the ASCS shifted significantly away from direct appropriations and toward transfers. As a result, inferences about the size of the ASCS's operations drawn from a cursory inspection of budget authority and outlay totals are misleading. As Table 4.2 indicates, appropriated budget authority was cut from $209 million in 1981 to zero in 1989, and the resulting outlays fell from $183 million to a small negative number. Despite these apparent reductions, the budgetary resources available to the bureau did not decline during the 1980s. In fact, its administrative budget grew by 80 percent during the eight-year period.

Growth was financed principally by a large increase in the funds transferred from the Commodity Credit Corporation (CCC). Under the government's accounting conventions, both the budget authority and the outlays for the transferred funds appear under the CCC programs. The CCC is primarily responsible for numerous large entitlement programs that in 1989 provided $10.6 billion in cash support for farmers.[17] In the federal government's budget for 1989, $619 million is included in the mandatory spending category; in fact, this amount was domestic discretionary spending.

The ASCS's budget growth during the 1980s was also financed by an increase in user fees. These fees are collected from farmers for services such as measurement and certification of farm acreage and crop yields and processing CCC loans. As in the case of the Patent and Trademark Office, these fees are used to defray the costs of the ASCS's operations without increasing reported budget authority and outlays.

The Federal Housing Administration (FHA), which insures mortgages for qualified buyers, thereby lowering the price of homes, is an hybrid example. The appropriation bill enacted in November 1989 raised the cap on single-family FHA mortgages from $101,250 to $124,875. This increase raised additional revenues from premiums paid by those who now qualify but would not have under the old cap, the funds to be used for administrative expenses.[18] As with the antitrust fee and other offsetting collections, the additional revenues did not add to reported outlays or budget authority.[19] Unlike the antitrust fee, these fees are not paid directly to the discretionary account; they are transferred from a mandatory account, that for the Federal Housing Administration Fund, to the discretionary Housing and Urban Development Department (HUD) administrative expenses account. Such transfers are substantial in amount; in 1989, for example, $382 million was transferred. But their budgetary treatment is such that they are classified as mandatory spending.

Other discretionary programs receive transfers from entitlements. For example, funds provided to the Food Stamp program have been transferred to the Department of Agriculture's Extension Service to cover the service's activities on behalf of the Food

Stamp program. Both the appropriated budget authority and outlays appear in the Food Stamp account and not in the Extension Service. Because of this convention, these transfers provided discretionary funding for the Extension Service without counting as discretionary budget authority.[20]

A final example of discretionary financing that is not counted as discretionary budget authority involves the recovery of prior-year obligations. This is money, usually budget authority, that was previously appropriated and obligated but will not be spent because it is not now needed. "Recovering" this prior-year money means that it can be returned to the program to be obligated and reduce the need for new budget authority by an equal amount.[21]

In summary, to measure the monetary size of government programs accurately, the total budgetary resources made available each year must be calculated. Simply measuring outlays or budget authority is misleading. Accordingly, other means of financing (offsetting receipts from the public, transfers from entitlement or from defense and international affairs programs, and recoveries of prior-year obligations) must be added to annually appropriated budget authority and limitations on obligations to obtain an accurate measure.

Defining Domestic Discretionary Programs

The Basic Concept of Domestic Discretionary Programs

Because the line between discretionary and mandatory spending is unclear, no universally agreed-upon definition of discretionary spending exists. In general, discretionary spending originates in an appropriations committee and is voted upon annually by Congress. The level of discretionary spending is not a function of a law that gives certain individuals, institutions, or states a right to federal funds. Authority for entitlement spending, alternatively, does not originate in an appropriations committee, nor is it usually determined by an annual vote of Congress. Instead, Congress passes an authorizing statute setting eligibility criteria for individuals or institutions for certain benefits. All those eligible receive the benefits as a matter of law until Congress rescinds that law or the law expires. The amount spent is effectively determined by the number who claim the benefits by which they are legally entitled under an authorizing statute and the amount to which each is entitled rather than by an appropriations act.

Constitutionally, there must be a grant of authority to spend before funds can be withdrawn from the Treasury. This requirement applies to all types of spending, whether for discretionary programs or entitlement or other mandatory spending.[22] Some entitlement programs, such as Social Security, and some of the other mandatory programs, such as interest on the public debt, are funded through permanent appropriations enacted in the past. For these programs, the payment of benefits or contractual obligations does not require annual congressional action. Other entitlements, "appropriated entitlements," including most welfare programs, are financed through current appropriations. The payment of benefits under these latter programs does require annual appropriations action by Congress. For appropriated entitlements, however, the required action is a pro forma event. The decisive point in the spending process occurred earlier when Congress passed the underlying authorizing statute that set benefit levels and eligibility requirements.

Despite appearances to the contrary, these seemingly clear bases for classification do not produce a universally agreed-upon list of discretionary programs. Fortunately, a list of domestic discretionary programs does not have to be developed anew. One already exists, as agreed to by Congress and the executive branch for use in carrying out the 1987 budget summit agreement. The negotiators chose to have a separate category for domestic discretionary spending as part of the agreement and agreed on its composition. The definition was modified by the agreement reached between the Bush administration and the congressional leadership in April 1989. This modified definition is used here, with the two exceptions noted next.

Exclusions

For most programs, the concept of budgetary resources accurately measures the domestic discretionary program level. For subsidized housing and credit programs, however, the use of this concept to measure changes in program size can be misleading. It is necessary, therefore, to exclude them from the universe of domestic discretionary programs if an accurate measure of the trend in domestic discretionary spending is to be developed.

Subsidized housing programs. The principal subsidized housing programs of the federal government are administered by the Department of Housing and Urban Development (HUD) and the Agriculture Department's Farmers Home Administration (FmHA). The HUD housing programs are of two generic types: "project-based" programs that provide subsidies to specific public or privately owned housing units and "tenant-based" programs that provide subsidies to eligible families or individuals. The FmHA programs are similar in nature, the principal program providing below-market interest rate mortgage loans to low-income families to purchase or repair new or existing housing as well as corporations, associations, state and local governments, and individuals to modernize or develop rental and cooperative housing for low-income and elderly persons.

A common feature of these programs is that they involve long-term commitments. Subsidies to owners or developers of low-income housing, for example, can involve contractual commitments of twenty or twenty-five years.

The basis for budgeting differs among these programs, however. The HUD housing programs follow the principles of traditional budgeting. Budget authority is allocated on a "full-funding" basis; that is, the maximum costs expected to be incurred over the life of the contract are budgeted initially.[23] Thus, budget authority represents an upper-bound estimate of the long-term cost to the government of the subsidy contract. For example, if the annual rental cost of a housing unit is $6,000 and the length of the contract is for ten years, the amount of budget authority required at the initiation of the contract is $60,000. As a result of this full-funding rule, *the number of new units a given amount of budget authority can finance depends upon the length of the contract.* Ten billion dollars of budget authority can finance twice as many new units if the length of the contract is ten years than if it is twenty years.

In the FmHA's rental-assistance programs, budget authority is not based on prospective long-term costs. Instead, it covers current-year obligations that have become due as a result of previous commitments. To illustrate, suppose that from a subsidy contract initiated previously, a housing unit is under contract in a given year with rental assistance payments of $6,000. The amount of budget authority required to cover the government's obligation for this unit in the current year would be $6,000. Because there is a considerable lag between the time a contract is initiated and the first rental-assistance payment, most if not all units subsidized in a given year were committed in prior years. Because the budget authority appropriated for a year is used to liquidate these prior-year obligations, the Appropriations Committee has little discretion in determining the amount of budget authority to be appropriated.

Finally, in the FmHA's direct mortgage-loan program, appropriated budget authority is determined on the basis of past lending activity, the amount appropriated used for "interest subsidies and losses sustained in prior years."[24] Again, the appropriators have little discretion in determining budget authority.

Although the budgetary treatments among housing programs differ, the programs' basic purpose is to make affordable housing available to low-income families and other specified individuals. To achieve this end, Congress increases the stock of housing by offering construction and other housing-development subsidies and reduces the cost of existing housing to low-income families by offering low-interest loans and rent subsidies. Besides budget authority, program size could be measured by the number of subsidized housing units in existence and the number of persons living in them. If either number increases, the size of the program may be said to have increased. As with all univariatae measures, however, these simple statistics are not without problems. For example, each measure ignores whether the magnitude of the "housing problem" is increasing or declining; that is, they are absolute, not relative measures. Moreover, neither measure incorporates changes in the size of the per-unit subsidy. Although the number of units or persons subsidized may increase, the size of the subsidy might decline. If so, the number of units would not necessarily measure the program size accurately.[25]

Table 4.3 compares budget authority, the number of subsidized units, and the number of persons served. For FmHA programs, both budget authority and the number of subsidized units increased, but the growth in the former far outstrips the growth in

TABLE 4.3
Housing Programs

	1981	1989	Change
HUD subsidized housing			
Budget authority ($ in millions)	30,170	6,989	−77%
Subsidized units ($ in thousands)	3,297	4,315	+31
Persons served (thousands)	8,244	10,788	+31
Average contract length (years)	21	11	−48
FMHA subsidized housing			
Budget authority ($ in millions)	562	3,837	+583%
Subsidized units ($ in thousands)	1,158	1,283	+11
Persons served (thousands)	2,894	3,208	+11
Total			
Budget authority ($ in millions)	30,732	10,826	−65%
Subsidized units ($ in thousands)	4,455	5,598	+26
Persons served (thousands)	11,138	13,996	+26

SOURCE: Budget authority was obtained from the U.S. OMB, *Budget*, FY 1991 and 1983. (The number of subsidized units and persons served were obtained from unpublished tables, U.S. OMB. The average contract length is computed as a budget authority weighted average among the various types of Section 8 contracts.) The source for the contract length is U.S. Dept. of Housing and Urban Development, *Budget Justification*, FY 1982 and 1990.

the latter. The sizable growth in budget authority is due primarily to a large increase in the spread between the Treasury cost of funds and the interest rate on FmHA loans from 1979 to 1987. This spread determines the amount that Congress must appropriate to cover the costs of its past commitments. But it bears little relationship to the stock of subsidized housing made available under the program.

For HUD programs, budget authority, the focus of much attention in the press, declined by nearly 80 percent during the 1980s. Yet, as with FmHA, budget authority does not measure program size. Despite the drop in budget authority, both the number of subsidized units and the number of persons served increased by almost 33 percent. Congress increased the number of units and individuals served while slashing budget authority by reducing the length of the typical housing contracts by about 50 percent between 1981 and 1989.[26]

Another source of the observed decline in budget authority was the shift from more expensive, project-based subsidies, which included construction costs, to less expensive vouchers that enable recipient families to receive subsidies for renting existing housing units.[27] A final source was the slowing of the growth of newly authorized units. In 1981, funds were provided for about 220,000 new housing units. In 1989, funds were provided for about 100,000.[28]

To summarize, no judgment is made here whether the size of subsidized housing programs has necessarily increased or decreased. Clearly, however, because of changes in the length of subsidized housing contracts, observed data on budget authority are uninformative regarding the direction and magnitude of any changes in program size during the 1980s. For this reason, subsidized housing programs must be excluded from the calculations.

Credit programs. Before the passage of credit reform legislation in 1990, credit programs are the second case in which budgetary resources fail to measure program size accurately. To understand why this is so, consider the financing of credit programs.

Most federal credit programs were financed through a revolving fund. Generally, payments of principal and interest on loans and other receipts of the fund are automatically available to finance new direct loans. Moreover, some programs can borrow from the Federal Financing Bank (FFB) or the public under permanent authority, and receipts from these sources also finance loan disbursements. Appropriated budget authority usually serves as only a residual means of financing—that is, for use when other sources are inadequate. Because it is a residual, the level of appropriated budget authority bears almost no relationship to the level of lending authorized in that year. The larger the dollar volume of loans repaid and the larger the receipts to the fund, the lower the level of appropriated budget authority required to finance a given amount of loan activity.

In three major Agriculture Department credit programs—the Rural Housing Insurance Fund, the Rural Development Insurance Fund, and the Agricultural Credit Insurance Fund—there was even less connection between appropriated budget authority and current program size during the 1980s. In each program, the amount of defaults, the amount of prior years' lending activity, and the spread between the loan and the Treasury interest rate on comparable loans determined the amount of appropriated budget author-

TABLE 4.4
Agricultural Credit Insurance Fund
($ in millions)

	1981	1989	Percent change
Direct loans:			
Limitation	$1,774	$1,569	−12%
Disbursements	1,691	1,030	−39
Loan guarantees:			
Limitations	$90	$2,775	+2,983%
New loans guaranteed	146	1,590	+989

SOURCE: U.S. OMB, *Budget* (Appendix), FY 1983 and 1991.

ity. Thus, budget authority reflected prior years' actions, not decisions on new loan activities.[29]

An alternative measure, such as a "direct loan limitation," which serves as an upper bound on funds that can be obligated for new loans, has similar problems. To illustrate the problems, consider the different treatments of direct and guaranteed loans during the 1980s. Obligations for direct loans result from agreements that the government will make a loan immediately or at some future time. Commitments for guaranteed loans result from the government's promise to guarantee the repayment of principal (and sometimes interest) on loans made by nonfederal lenders. Before the 1990s, loan guarantees, unlike direct loans, did not require obligational authority or federal disbursements when the guarantee is authorized. This difference in budgetary treatment allowed for a total reduction in the recorded direct-loan limitation, with much less change in program effect, by simply changing loans from direct to guaranteed but making the guaranteed loans as identical to the direct loans as possible. Yet a dollar of guarantee did not equal a dollar of direct loan. Even a shift from a direct to a 100 percent guaranteed loan may not provide the borrower with terms as favorable, because the direct loans frequently have an interest rate lower than that for guarantees.

The measurement problems created by the opportunity to shift loans from direct to guaranteed are not merely of hypothetical interest. Table 4.4 shows the shift in loans for the Agricultural

Credit Insurance Fund. This fund finances operating loans to farmers. In nominal dollars, direct loans fell sharply, but loan guarantees increased by even higher amounts. As the data indicate, use of direct-loan limitations would severely misrepresent changes in the magnitude of operating loans available to farmers through federal credit programs.

A more general problem is that loan programs cannot be treated on a par with discretionary procurement or grant programs. Although loans frequently have an element of a government grant—for example, by charging the borrower a below-market interest rate—to the extent they are repaid, they are fundamentally different from grants. A dollar loaned is not a dollar of taxpayers' money spent. The taxpayers' contribution includes the market value of the subsidy to the loan recipient, which includes consideration of potential repayment.

The problems of measuring loan programs have long been recognized and have been the subject of considerable debate during the past twenty-five years.[30] The 1967 President's Commission on Budget Concepts, whose recommendations led to the creation of today's unified budget, discussed the treatment of credit programs at length. In the early 1970s, their treatment was reconsidered during the debates over the establishment of the Federal Financing Bank (FFB) and the enactment of the Congressional Budget and Impoundment Control Act.[31] In the latter part of the 1980s, the budgetary treatment of credit programs came under scrutiny again, and in 1990 it was overhauled by the 1990 bipartisan budget agreement.

Credit reform legislation in 1990 changed the measurement of all future loans to equal (in theory) the subsidy value of the loan. However, data on these values for loans made during the 1980s have not been computed, nor can they be from published government data. Hence, all loan programs have been excluded from our analysis.

Empirical Results

The federal government does not publish comprehensive information on the total amount made available to domestic discretionary programs for obligation each year. The *Budget of the United States*

Government contains information derived from reports prepared by the Treasury and the Office of Management and Budget on the amount of enacted budget authority and outlays at the agency, bureau, and budget account levels for the fiscal year just completed. In recent years, it has also included a historical series on these two measures at a more aggregate level. In the legislative branch, the House and Senate budget committees issue reports showing budget authority and outlay totals at the budget function classification or congressional committee levels. The Congressional Budget Office, in addition to publishing some program-level data on budget authority and outlays, also provides a historical series of outlays by major budget category, including national defense, nondefense discretionary, and entitlements.

The information needed to measure budgetary resources is available in the appendix to the *Budget of the United States Government.*[32] The Program and Financing schedule in the appendix identifies the various means by which each budget account is financed, including offsetting collections from the public, recovery of prior-year obligations, budget authority, transfers from other budget accounts, and balances from prior years. Total budgetary resources derived from the first three of these categories can be obtained simply by adding together the amounts shown for each.

Transfers, however, present a problem. The account from which the transfer is made is not identified, although transfers from trust funds are shown separately from transfers from federal fund accounts (primarily general-fund accounts). Hence, transfers of budget authority from entitlements, defense, or international affairs programs cannot always be distinguished from transfers from other domestic discretionary programs on the basis of the information contained in any published government document. To count transfers from other domestic programs as budgetary resources by the program receiving the transfer would double-count these funds because they are also treated as budget authority for the account to which they have been appropriated. On the other hand, failure to count transfers from entitlements, defense, or international affairs programs would underestimate the total amount available for obligation for domestic discretionary programs.

In our construction of the data, transfers were counted as budgetary resources by a domestic discretionary program receiving the transfer only if the transfer could be identified from other information contained in the appendix as originating from an entitlement, defense, or international affairs program. Because not all such transfers can be identified, the measure of domestic discretionary budgetary resources used in this chapter almost certainly understates the actual total. Because the frequency and amount of transfers appear to have increased in recent years, this measure also likely understates the growth in domestic discretionary spending.

One drawback of the budget appendix is that it does not provide final totals on enacted levels of all limitations on obligations (sometimes referred to as limits on administrative expenses). To identify these enacted levels, all enacted regular appropriation bills, continuing resolutions, and supplemental appropriation bills signed into law during the years of the inquiry were examined. These enacted obligation limitations were combined with other means of financing available in the appendix to obtain the total new budgetary resources made available each year.

Aggregate Results

Table 4.5 presents the total budgetary resources for 1981, 1982, and 1989, divided into budget authority, obligation limitations and limitations of administrative expenses, and other means of financing. The results show that in the aggregate budgetary resources grew slightly less than inflation during the 1980s. Although the largest form of budgetary resources, budget authority, grew by 5 percent less than inflation, the other forms of budgetary resources, which were subject to less scrutiny in the budgetary process than budget authority, grew substantially more than inflation.

Consistent with the treatment in the President's budget, budgetary resources for the Employment Service, administration of state unemployment insurance programs, and Medicare contractor payments are treated as transfers from funds rather than limits on obligations. This treatment does not affect the totals.

The virtual freeze in budgetary resources between 1981 and 1989 masks the actual trends of those eight years. As Table 4.5 shows, programs were cut dramatically between 1981 and 1982, but in the next seven years inflation-adjusted budgetary resources grew by about 14 percent. (Budget authority grew by nearly 13

TABLE 4.5

Budgetary Resources by Type

	1981	1982	1989	Percent change, 1981–89	Percent change, 1981–82	Percent change, 1982–89
			Nominal dollars			
Budget authority	107.6	96.9	137.8	+28.1	−9.9	+42.2
Limits on obligation	13.8	13.7	20.3	+47.1	−0.7	+48.2
Other means of financing	5.7	6.2	9.8	+71.9	+8.8	+58.1
TOTAL	127.1	116.8	167.9	+32.1	−8.1	+43.7
			Constant 1989 dollars			
Budget authority	145.2	122.1	137.8	−5.1	−15.9	+12.9
Limits on obligation	18.6	17.3	20.3	+9.1	−7.0	+17.3
Other means of financing	7.7	7.8	9.8	+27.3	+1.3	+25.6
TOTAL	171.5	147.2	167.9	−2.1	−14.2	+14.1

SOURCE: Budget authority and means of financing data from U.S. OMB, *Budget* (Appendix), FY 1983, 1984, and 1991. Limits on obligations are obtained from Budget appendix when provided and from individual appropriation bills otherwise.

percent.) In what areas these reductions and increases occurred is the subject addressed next.

Disaggregated Results

Within the eight-year constant-dollar freeze on domestic discretionary spending, a significant reordering of budgetary priorities took place. To illustrate the nature and magnitude of the changes, the data have been organized into governmental bureaus. Bureaus are typically administrative units within agencies or departments, and they usually administer more than one government program. Tables 4.6 and 4.7 present bureau-level changes in budgetary resources between 1981 and 1989. Table 4.6 provides data on all bureaus with more than $1 billion in budgetary resources that experienced inflation-adjusted growth in excess of 20 percent.[33] Table 4.7 provides the same information for all such bureaus whose budget experienced 20 percent reductions. Together, the bureaus listed in these two tables compose nearly 60 percent of all domestic discretionary spending in 1989.

Increases. The data provided in Table 4.6 indicate that the increases in funding levels in the 1980s were broad-based. Fifteen

TABLE 4.6
Major Bureau Budget Increases
(billions of 1989 dollars)

	Budgetary resources		
	1981	1989	Percent change
Federal Prison System	$0.5	$1.6	206%
Immigration and Naturalization Service	0.5	1.1	120
Court of Appeals	0.6	1.1	83
Internal Revenue Service	3.3	5.2	58
Handicapped Education[a]	1.4	2.1	50
National Institute of Health	4.9	7.2	47
House and Senate[b]	0.7	1.0	43
National Aeronautical Space Agency	7.8	10.9	40
Alcohol, Drug Abuse, and Mental Health Administration	1.3	1.8	39
National Park Service	0.8	1.1	38
National Science Foundation	1.4	1.9	36
Federal Aviation Administration	4.8	6.5	35
Federal Medicare/Health Care Financing Administration[c]	1.3	1.7	31
Veterans Medical Care[d]	9.3	11.6	25
Environmental Protection Agency	4.6	5.6	22

SOURCE: U.S. OMB, *Budget* (Appendix), FY 1983 and 1993. (Data for 1981 have been adjusted for inflation using the fiscal-year GNP delator [*Budget*, FY 1991, p. A-283]. During the years 1981–89, economy-wide prices rose 35 percent.)

[a]Includes assistance to Special Institutions.

[b]Includes all discretionary individual and joint House and Senate accounts.

[c]Includes federal employees' salaries and expenses and payments to medicare contractors who administer the program at the state and local level.

[d]Includes salaries and expenses, research, and construction.

bureaus with budgets of $1 billion or more registered inflation-adjusted increases of at least 20 percent.[34] These bureaus have responsibility for a wide spectrum of government activities, ranging from long-standing activities like tax collection to more recent activities like environmental protection. Although much has been made of the large growth in the defense budget during the Reagan administration, the budgets of twelve of the bureaus listed in Table 4.6 grew faster than the Department of Defense budget.[35]

The list of bureaus in Table 4.6 also suggests that during the 1980s bureau budgets were quite responsive to emerging issues. The substantial growth in the budget of the Immigration and Natu-

TABLE 4.7
Major Bureau Budget Reductions
(billions of 1989 dollars)

	Budgetary resources		
	1981	1989	Percent change
Postal Service	$1.8	$0.4	−78%
Community Planning and Development	6.1	2.0	−67
Federal Railroad Administration	2.0	0.7	−65
Energy Programs	12.8	6.3	−51
Employment and Training Admin. (CETA)	13.6	6.7	−51
Urban Mass Transit Administration	6.3	3.3	−48
Family Support Administration[a]	4.2	2.3	−45
Army Corps of Engineers	4.1	3.2	−22

SOURCE: U.S. OMB, *Budget* (Appendix), FY 1983 and 1991. (Data for 1981 have been adjusted for inflation using the fiscal year GNP delator [*Budget*, FY 1991, p. A-283]. During the years 1981–89, economy-wide prices rose 35 percent.)

[a]Bureau includes low-income home energy assistance program, refugee aid, community services block grant, and work incentives program.

ralization Service reflects the widespread concern over illegal immigration. This concern had been building since the latter part of the 1970s and led to reform legislation in 1986 that produced the large growth in the service's budget. Likewise, the desire for increases in revenue to reduce the large budget deficits influenced the growth in the Internal Revenue Service budget.[36] The crises involving AIDS and drug abuse during the 1980s prompted substantial increases in the budgets of the National Institutes of Health and the Alcohol, Drug Abuse, and Mental Health Administration.

Finally, the data also suggest the important role the President's priorities play in determining the allocation of federal funds among competing claimants. The largest areas of domestic budget growth were in bureaus involved in the traditional functions of the federal government, such as administering immigration laws and operating the federal court and penal systems. The budgets of the National Aeronautical Space Agency and the National Science Foundation also registered hefty increases. The President and other administration officials actively supported substantial increases in the budgets of each of these bureaus throughout most of the 1980s.[37]

At least two other areas that registered significant increases not shown in Table 4.6 are worth noting. Federal spending on highways grew by almost 3 percent in real terms (nearly 40 percent before adjusting for inflation). This growth was financed largely by the five-cent-per-gallon increase in the federal gasoline tax enacted in 1982. Also, in an era when the federal role in education is said to have been restrained, the budget of the Department of Education grew by 14 percent in real terms. Increases in the department's budget occurred at almost every level. As noted in Table 4.6, education for the handicapped increased by 50 percent. Moreover, elementary and secondary education programs grew by 11 percent, and higher education programs, led by a growth in Pell Grant funding, increased by 14 percent.

Decreases. Some bureaus suffered major declines in budgetary resources. The reductions were heavily concentrated in a few large bureaus. The eight bureaus listed in Table 4.7 account for 76 percent of all budget cuts. The combined constant-dollar cut in these eight bureaus totaled $26 billion. It is interesting to note that when these eight bureaus are excluded, there was 19 percent real growth in the entire remainder of the domestic discretionary budget.

Most of the large programs that make up the reductions reported in Table 4.7 have two characteristics in common. First, with the exception of the Postal Service and energy programs, the programs served primarily local community needs rather than any national purpose. Second, for various reasons, many of the reductions should have been expected. Funding for some programs, such as the Postal Service and refugee aid (part of the Family Support Administration), could be reduced without affecting the program's normal activities. With the passage of the energy crisis from the American economy during the 1980s, the high levels of funding for certain energy programs no longer enjoyed wide support. Finally, many programs were in a relative sense weak claimants on the budget because both President Carter at the end of his administration and President Reagan throughout his tenure had proposed cutbacks.

The largest percentage decrease was registered by the appropriation for the Postal Service to offset revenues lost when it charges certain customers a below-normal postal rate. Because the appropriation is only one means by which the Postal Service can obtain funds from the federal budget, this reduction is somewhat illusory.

The Postal Service also has the right to borrow at subsidized interest rates from the Treasury. By using this authority, the Postal Service can substitute borrowed Treasury funds for appropriated funds.[38] Because the Postal Service borrows from the Treasury under permanent authority to borrow, this source of funds amounts to substituting a mandatory expenditure for a discretionary one.

The large reductions in community planning and development, the Urban Mass Transit Authority, and the Army Corps of Engineers were primarily in "bricks and mortar" programs that largely benefited local areas. In community planning and development, funding for the Urban Development Action Grant program was terminated (about $1 billion in 1981) and community development block grants were sharply cut back. The nearly $1 billion (constant dollars) cut in the Army Corps of Engineers budget represents a reduction in the rate of development of various types of water projects such as harbor dredging, flood control, and dam construction and renovation. In the mass transit programs, operating subsidies to municipal governments were cut back sharply, and federal approval of matching grants to these governmental entities for construction of new projects was delayed. The more than $7 billion in cuts in these programs underlies the charge that federal programs for public infrastructure were gutted during the 1980s. In part because the programs that suffered severe reductions in these categories serve almost an exclusively local purpose, they were targeted for reduction.

The third area of deep reductions occurred in various programs whose rise and fall is directly related to the energy crisis. More than $6 billion (constant dollars) in reductions occurred in the Department of Energy's energy supply and research and development programs and in its strategic petroleum reserve. An additional $1 billion (constant dollars) reduction took place in the Department of Health and Human Service low-income home energy program, listed in Table 4.7 under the Family Support Administration. The growth, indeed the mere existence, of these programs resulted from the meteoric rise in energy prices during the latter half of the 1970s. When energy prices began to collapse in the early 1980s, so did support for many energy programs.[39]

The $6.5 billion (constant dollars) cut in the Labor Department's Employment and Training Administration reflects primarily the termination of the public service employment program. The re-

TABLE 4.8

Distribution of Major Changes in Domestic Discretionary Spending

(in billions of dollars)

	1981	1989[a]	Amount change	Percent change
		Nominal dollars		
Bureaus with major reductions	37.7	24.9	−12.8	−40.1
Bureaus with major increases	32.0	60.4	+28.4	+88.8
All other bureaus	57.4	82.6	+25.2	+43.9
TOTAL	127.1	167.9	+40.8	+32.1
		Constant 1989 dollars		
Bureaus with major reductions	50.9	24.9	−26.0	−51.1
Bureaus with major increases	43.2	60.4	+17.2	+39.8
All other bureaus	77.4	82.6	+5.2	+6.7
TOTAL	171.5	167.9	−3.6	−2.1

SOURCE: U.S. OMB, *Budget* (Appendix), FY 1983 and 1991.
[a]Inflation 1981–89 = 35%.

maining (after subtracting low-income energy) $800 million (constant dollars) reduction listed under the Family Support Administration occurred in the refugee assistance program. The 1981 level from which the reduction is measured was the result of a onetime funding increase after the sharp influx of refugees from the Mariel boat lift.

Table 4.8 combines information provided in the two previous tables to illustrate the extent to which budget reductions were concentrated and increases broad-based. The eight bureaus identified as receiving the largest budget reductions accounted in 1981 for about 30 percent of all domestic discretionary spending. Programs in these bureaus were cut by about 50 percent in real terms. Programs in the remaining 70 percent of the budget grew by 19 percent after adjusting for inflation.

Conclusion

Our analysis has demonstrated that the widely held view that during the 1980s nonentitlement domestic spending was "pared to the bone" is incorrect. In the aggregate, domestic discretionary spending increased nearly at the rate of overall inflation in the economy. The period 1981–89 is more appropriately characterized as one year of deep budget cuts, 1982, followed by rapid budget growth. By the end of the eight-year period, this budget growth had restored aggregate domestic discretionary spending to its 1981 constant-dollar level. Deep budget cuts sustained over the eight years were highly concentrated in a few areas of government activity, such as energy programs, water projects, public service employment, and local development projects. These programs are not generally included in lists of national priorities compiled by advocates of increased spending. The distribution of budget increases, on the other hand, tended to be broad-based and included many areas labeled as priorities in the current debate over government spending, such as antidrug programs, basic science research, education, and environmental programs.

The prevailing wisdom about aggregate nonentitlement domestic spending reductions is wrong because it is based upon an incorrect understanding of conventional budget data. For many programs, the most commonly used data, budget authority and outlays, do not accurately measure the total funds Congress makes available for obligation. When a proper measure of the amount available for obligation is used, the true size of budget growth becomes apparent.

Our analysis is important with regard to the current budget debate. Many advocates of increased spending for domestic programs assert that because total nonentitlement domestic spending was reduced during the 1980s, some restoration of total budgetary resources is in order. Our analysis reveals that the basis for this view is erroneous. Although there are certainly compelling reasons for budget increases in certain domestic discretionary programs, prior reductions in the aggregate amount of resources appropriated for them is not one of them.

Finally, the fact that the conventional wisdom about what happened to nonentitlement domestic spending could be so wrong means that important improvements should be made in the way that the executive branch and the congressional committees report budget information. Given the widespread use of means other than budget authority to finance government programs, the almost exclusive focus on budget authority by the President's budget and congressional budget documents belongs to a bygone era. More meaningful measures of the resources made available for government activities should be developed.

5

The Study of Microbudgeting

ALLEN SCHICK

MOST persons who prepare or implement budgets are concerned with particular programs or items. Only a few work on the totals, and when they do, it is usually to add up the various pieces. Microbudgeters populate government agencies, which run the programs and spend the money, and Congress, which decides who gets what. In practice, microbudgeting almost always preoccupies budget makers, the exceptions being those interludes when extraordinary attention is paid to the totals. But if practice has been dominated by a microbudgeting perspective, the opposite has been true of the *study* of budgeting. With the breakdown of macrobudgeting, however, there has been a surge of interest in how particularistic behavior affects the conduct and results of budgeting.

The Practice of Microbudgeting

Microbudgeting is the study of the impacts of institutions and information on actions and outcomes. It is the study of how the behavior of those who make budgets is shaped by the institutions in which they work and the information they have at hand. Budgeting is not conducted in a vacuum; every participant has a role and data. These may be formally prescribed in rules and procedures, though they often arise informally from the interests and interactions of budget makers.

Chapters 3 and 4 in this volume deal with information; Chapter 2 examines institutions. Information refers to the content and structure of the data available to budget makers as well as the way budget actions are scored and reported. Accounting rules, baseline computations, and the assumptions used to compute the impacts of actions are major pieces of the informational map of budgeting. Institutions refer to the characteristic roles of participants and the formal and informal rules guiding their behavior. The reconciliation process, sequestration procedures, and jurisdictional structure of congressional committees are prominent institutional features of budgeting. Three basic institutional issues are discussed below: (1) presidential versus congressional budget roles; (2) the dispersion of spending jurisdiction among congressional committees; and (3) the behavior of the appropriations committees.

Presidential versus Congressional Roles

Budgeting in Congress is not a clone of budgeting in the executive branch. While it is the weaker branch in dealing with the totals, Congress dominates the microbudget. The dispersion of budgetary jurisdiction in Congress enables committees to concentrate on the parts of the budget that matter most to them. Although no committee has legislative control of the whole budget, each has a strong incentive to be vigilant regarding the matters in its jurisdiction.

The decentralized structure of Congress gives it many advantages when the two branches lock horns on particular matters. The White House does not have enough eyes and ears to monitor everything that Congress does to the budget or enough political capital to challenge every unwanted provision in appropriations bills or other measures. A member of Congress is much more likely to care about matters affecting his state or district than the President is, and much more likely to actively fight in behalf of his constituents. In microbudgeting, the White House must pick its fights very selectively, which is a way of saying that it must yield on most matters of interest to Congress. If he cares enough about a particular issue and is willing to invest sufficient attention, the President can prevail. The problem for him, however, is that he cannot care about everything in his budget, nor can he confront Congress every time it inserts an offensive provision into a budget-related measure.

The characteristic response of presidents to the inherent mismatch between the two branches on microbudgeting has been to turn the other cheek on small changes made by Congress, provided that they do not imperil the President's overall control of the budget. In the past, the President's task was simplified by reliance on party discipline. With Congress following his policy lead, the President could be confident that legislated changes would be manageable.

In the 1980s, however, the President became more involved in microbudgeting at the very time that governmental control was divided and Congress was asserting its independence. Reagan could have avoided confrontation by going along with Congress and limiting his budgetary objectives to incremental changes. Instead, he sought to wrest control of the domestic agenda from Congress and to reorder national priorities. Although he scored a few impressive victories at the start, over the full term of his presidency Reagan was no match for a Congress organized to serve microbudgetary interests. When Reagan challenged Congress by threatening to veto its budget legislation, Congress compelled him to retreat by packaging numerous provisions, including hotly contested items and provisions the President wanted, in omnibus continuing resolutions or other essential legislation. With only two options—to sign or to veto the entire measure—the President's microbudgetary influence was diminished.

The Dispersion of Budgetary Power in Congress

During its two-hundred-year history, Congress has gone through cycles of concentration and dispersion with respect to budgetary (and legislative) power. There have been periods when budgetary jurisdiction was concentrated in a few committees and other periods when power was widely distributed. The present period can be described as having a high degree of committee fragmentation, combined with efforts to coordinate budget policy through the budget process and party leaderships.

As John Cogan shows in Chapter 2, the dispersion of budgetary power is indicated by the number of House and Senate committees that have direct spending jurisdiction and by the declining share of total expenditures controlled by the appropriations committees. This trend has been accompanied by another development noted in Cogan's research: the growing percentage of federal revenues earmarked to trust funds. In 1950, trust funds accounted for only 10 percent of total receipts; today, they hold almost 40 percent. The rise in trust funds is associated with another postwar trend: the growing portion of the budget spent on entitlements and other mandated payments.

The degree of legislative dispersion has a pronounced impact on the relationship between the budget's parts and the totals. As legislative budgetary power has been more widely distributed, it is increasingly difficult for Congress to control the totals. Cogan argues that the increased dispersion of spending jurisdiction in Congress has driven up federal expenditures and the deficit. Drawing a lesson from the "tragedy of the commons" (an often-cited explanation for the despoilment of the environment), Cogan shows how individual committees acting in their self-interest produce budget outcomes that few in Congress want. That is, if each committee succeeds in getting more for its program, total spending and the deficit will be higher than any committee wants. This problem is mitigated when spending control is concentrated in the appropriations committees because these committees have both the incentive and the capacity to produce acceptable totals.

Cogan buttresses his argument with evidence of changes in congressional spending jurisdiction in earlier periods. Federal expenditures and the deficit rose late in the nineteenth century when jurisdiction over half the spending bills was shifted from the appropriations committees to various authorizing committees. But spending the deficit abated in the 1920s, when jurisdiction was restored to the appropriations committees.[1]

Cogan's analysis of the dispersion of committee jurisdiction is closely linked to the growth of trust funds, the other budgetary trend identified earlier. In principle, the rise in either trust receipts or mandatory outlays could alone explain the growth in federal spending without reference to the way Congress is organized. Inasmuch as most of the growth in federal spending has been concentrated in trust funds and mandatory programs—the two categories overlap—it would seem that budget trends can be explained without having to consider the impact of Congress's committee structure. Nevertheless, a strong case can be made that the trend in trust funds and mandatory payments is directly related to the dispersion of congressional spending power.

My argument runs as follows: The dispersion of spending power could be accomplished either (1) by changing the House or Senate rules to transfer jurisdiction from the appropriations committees to other committees or (2) by changing the character of expenditures so that other committees gain effective control of spending bills. The first approach was used a century ago, when the appropriations committees were divested of more than half their bills; the second has been used in recent times by various legislative committees to obtain "backdoor" spending jurisdiction over particular programs.[2] Shifting from general funds to trust funds and from discretionary appropriations to entitlements has been the principal contemporary means of enlarging the budgetary jurisdiction of legislative committees at the expense of the appropriations committees. (The term *general fund* used here corresponds to *federal funds* in the U.S. budget, though the latter also contains some special funds.)

In the case of trust funds, the chief beneficiaries have been the House Ways and Means Committee and the Senate Finance Committee, which have jurisdiction over virtually all federal tax legislation. When they formulate revenue measures, these committees must decide whether the additional money should be deposited in the general fund or earmarked to a trust fund.

The shift from the general fund to trust funds has not been budget-neutral. The tax-writing committees have a strong incentive to favor trust funds and to starve the general fund. It is not accidental that Congress has maintained most of the trust funds in a strong financial condition. The annual surplus of all trust funds now exceeds $100 billion and is likely to grow in the years ahead as the Social Security funds build up huge balances.[3] If these funds were to get into trouble, the affected committees would have to either cut programs or raise taxes; when the funds are in a strong condition, as the Social Security and highway funds generally have been, the committees can use the available resources to expand programs. Overall, the growth of trust funds has probably added to total spending but lowered the deficit.

As the biggest trust fund, Social Security sheds light on the importance of surpluses in fueling program expansion. The process is not particularly complicated, though as chronicled by Martha Derthick in *Policymaking for Social Security*, managing it requires considerable political skill. The process works as follows: Using conservative actuarial assumptions, the guardians of Social Security's fiscal health would insist that a rise in social insurance premiums was essential to keep the trust funds in sound financial order. The incremental resources would then make room for program expansion, which would in turn strengthen the case for another raise in the premiums. The upshot was that the Social Security wage base and tax rate grew apace with program expansion.[4]

The impact of recent trends on the general fund has been substantially different. The tax-writing committees have little incentive to provide general revenues or to keep this fund in balance. From their vantage point, generating additional revenue for the general fund simply gives other committees more money to spend. At times their attitude seems to be that the best way to control general-fund spending is to underprovide for it. Evidence of this behavior can be found in the fact that general-fund receipts declined from 15 percent of GNP in 1960 to only 12 percent in 1990. This is not a small drop; in current dollars, it exceeds $160 billion a year. But the downtrend in revenues has not been matched by the trend in expenditures. During the past thirty years, as general revenues receded 3 percent relative to GNP, general expenditures rose 3 percent. It appears, therefore, that constraining general revenues has had little impact on expenditures but has added to the deficit. On a combined basis, the treatment of the general fund and trust funds has probably added to both expenditures and the deficit.

The shift from discretionary to mandatory expenditures has had a similar cause and similar budgetary effects. This shift has been one of the means by which spending power has been dispersed in Congress. The appropriations committees rule the roost when decisions are made for discretionary accounts. They have a free hand in recommending how much should be provided, and they are not bound—though they may be influenced—by the preferences of authorizing committees. Other committees, however, can take budgetary power from them by mandating expenditures in authorizing legislation. Even if the appropriations committees retain nominal jurisdiction, as they do for the many appropriated entitlements, effective spending control passes from them to authorizing committees. From the perspective of authorizing committees, the rise in entitlements is not just a matter of shoring up the economic status of Americans but a favored method for redistributing budgetary power in Congress.

The behavior of congressional committees in switching from discretionary to mandatory programs does suggest the "tragedy of the commons" discussed by Cogan. Although committees may prefer that Congress have effective control of federal spending, a committee enhances its own power when it establishes entitlements that weaken the overall budgetary capacity of Congress.

Because the contemporary dispersion of budgetary power has been accomplished by changing the character of federal expenditures rather than simply by altering House or Senate rules, it may be difficult to reverse. There are few instances where entitlements have been converted to discretionary programs, and fewer yet where revenues have been switched from trust funds to the general fund. The self-correcting mechanisms that enabled Congress to consolidate spending power in the appropriations committees during the 1920s may not suffice this time around. If this is so, the adverse impacts of budgetary fragmentation in Congress—difficult-to-control expenditures and chronically high deficits—may be a structural rather than a cyclical problem.

The Appropriations Committees: Guardians as Spenders

In considering whether recent financial strains might persist, one must take into account not only the actions of authorizing committees but those of the appropriations committees as well. A key to understanding these committees is the marked imbalance between general-fund revenue and expenditure. One would expect that as general receipts declined relative to GNP, the appropriations committees would have adjusted to this condition and seen to it that general expenditures also trended down. Part of the explanation of why this did not happen is embedded in the shift from discretionary to mandatory programs. While some of the biggest mandatory programs (Social Security and part of Medicare) are trust-funded, most entitlements and virtually all interest payments are financed by the general fund. These mandatory payments, which are not easily adjusted to revenue trends, have consumed a rising share of general-fund resources. Net interest payments now amount to almost 30 percent of general receipts, compared to less than 10 percent in 1960.[5] During this period, entitlements also have claimed a rising share of the general fund.

However, the imbalance in the general fund cannot be fully explained by the actions of authorizing committees in establishing or expanding entitlements financed out of the general fund. The appropriations committees control the approximately 35 percent of the budget that is spent on discretionary programs. The biggest chunk of discretionary money is for defense; over the years, this part of the budget has gone through cyclical swings corresponding to changes in international conditions and public opinion. Over the full postwar period, however, discretionary domestic spending has trended up. In fact, the study by Cogan and Muris reported in Chapter 4 found that even during the 1980s discretionary domestic spending just about kept even with inflation. After declining in the first half of the 1980s, discretionary domestic spending escalated later in the decade, a trend that has continued in the 1990s. Adjusted for inflation, this category of expenditure was 30 percent higher in fiscal 1993 than it had been six years earlier.

To explain the pattern in discretionary spending, it is necessary to examine the behavior of the appropriations committees. It is reasonable to surmise that the dispersal of congressional budgetary jurisdiction has affected not only those committees that gained backdoor spending authority but the appropriations committees as well. These committees know that if they take a hard line on spending, they risk further loss of jurisdiction through the shift of programs to entitlements or trust funds. The appropriations committees must spend enough on discretionary programs to show congressional colleagues that there is no need to take control away from them. To make a convincing case, these committees must be spenders of federal dollars.

This has always been the case in spending on "pork," the project money channeled by appropriations members to their states or districts. There is some evidence that the spending proclivities of the appropriations committees have matured from pork to programs, from benefits earmarked to particular geographic constituencies to resources made available nationally. The pork has remained, of course. In dollar terms, the amount of grant and project money earmarked to designated states or districts is probably at an all-time high, but its budget share has declined relative to program expenditures. One of the important differences between pork and programs is that the latter tend to be more expensive because the benefits are spread much more broadly.

While no single factor induced the appropriations committees to take a more accommodating posture toward program expenditure, rules changes mandated by the House Democratic Caucus in the 1970s certainly were a major influence.[6] Over time, the traditional concept of appropriations as restraints on executive authority to spend public funds has been supplemented by the concept of appropriations as mandates to spend. The evolution of impoundment from an unregulated practice in which the President (or an executive agency) withheld appropriations into a strict statutory procedure that virtually compels the full expenditure of available funds provides telling evidence of the changed status of appropriations.[7] Further evidence of this turnaround can be found in the growing practice by the appropriations committees of prescribing staffing minimums for certain programs instead of the once customary ceilings on personnel.[8]

The adjustment to a more programmatic attitude has not always been easy for congressional appropriators. These committees have typically preferred measured, incremental growth, not the leaps sometimes taken by the authorizing committees.[9] Incremental growth allows the appropriations committees to preserve their self-image of guarding the treasury while steadily providing more federal resources. It also allows them to bring home the bacon without breaching the budget totals. Because pork is relatively cheap, these committees can distribute a lot of it while balancing their guardian and spending roles.

This behavior, however, requires a cooperative President who regularly asks for more money than was provided the year before. As long as the President requests increases, the appropriations committees can behave both as guardians (providing less than was requested) and spenders (providing more than was voted for the previous year). Thus a cooperative President enables these committees to have it both ways: they can characterize the same action as a budget cut and a program increase.

Because this relationship gives each side what it cares about most, it has persisted for many years under varying political and fiscal conditions. It enables the President to control macrobudgetary policy while giving the appropriations committees substantial discretion to rearrange spending priorities. Although many presidents have railed against the appropriations committees (or Congress) for busting the budget or compelling wasteful expenditures, most knew that the earmarks and add-ons rarely amounted to more than a few percentage points.

For generations, the secret of appropriations power has been in the details of the budget. These committees are schooled in draining big issues of policy divisiveness by reducing them to routine questions of a little more versus a little less. They have usually been discomforted by efforts to blow up incremental spending issues into major policy disputes. They understand that their main task is to get spending bills enacted and that unlike other committees, they never have the option of doing nothing. If they add a little pork or program expenditure to the budget, they still want the totals to be acceptable.

Ronald Reagan disturbed this comfortable relationship in 1981 by challenging the appropriations committees for control of microbudgetary policy. Reagan wanted to downsize government, and he understood that by playing the incremental game and asking for more, he would be giving Congress license to spend more. Congress would get credit for cutting his budget, but domestic spending would be much higher than he thought it should be. Reagan therefore broke with past presidential practice by asking for less discretionary domestic funds than had been appropriated for the previous year. For many programs, the President demanded outright termination or substantial retrenchment. Reagan's budget took away the appropriations committees' expedient practice of cutting back while spending more. Measured against the Reagan request, any increment to the previous year's level would be an addition, often a hefty one, to the President's budget as well.

Reagan got his way, in the beginning. Using blitzkrieg tactics during the early months of his presidency. Reagan won enactment of a reconciliation bill that according to estimates made at that time, reduced authorizations for numerous domestic programs by $130 billion over a three-year period.[10] This legislation forced the appropriations committees to mark up many of their fiscal 1982 spending bills below the previous year's level.

By fall 1981, however, the appropriations committees had regrouped, and they successfully withstood White House pressure for further cuts that year and deep cuts in subsequent Reagan budgets. To help their cause, they prevailed on congressional colleagues to restrict the reconciliation process to mandatory programs, which meant that it would no longer be used to trim discretionary appropriations.[11] It is generally assumed that for the remainder of the Reagan presidency, the two sides held each other to a standoff. According to this view, although some cuts were restored and domestic appropriations regularly exceeded the President's request, Congress did not recover what was surrendered in 1981. But in Chapter 4 John Cogan and Timothy Muris draw a significantly different picture of budgetary outcomes in the 1980s. On the basis of a careful account-by-account reconstruction of the data, Cogan and Muris conclude that after 1981, available resources rose faster than inflation. For the full decade, resources just about kept even with inflation.

Why is the popular view of what happened in the 1980s so markedly different from what actually occurred? A big part of the answer is that as the budget situation worsened and conflict with the President persisted, the appropriations committees often turned to financing schemes that understated the true amount of available resources. Despite Reagan, they wanted to maintain their self-image of fiscal prudence while providing more than the President had requested. The easiest way to cut spending and to increase program funding would have been to compute appropriations decisions against the baseline. But unlike the budget committees (and many authorizing committees), which used inflated baselines to show that they were cutting the budget, the appropriations committees preferred to rely on actual rather than assumed numbers.[12] Instead of using baselines, the appropriations committees compared their actions to the "Section 302" allocations made through the congressional budget process. In addition, they sometimes resorted to complex financing arrangements that often understated the new budget resources flowing to particular accounts.

Section 302 allocations, which are based on the adopted budget resolution, generally set aside more money for domestic appropriations than has been requested by President Reagan. By staying within their Section 302 allocations, the appropriations committees could claim they were being fiscally responsible, even though the amount they provided exceeded the President's request.

The second means of spending more while keeping within the budget was to use some of the financing methods described by

Cogan and Muris. These include transferring funds between accounts, increased reliance on offsetting collections such as user charges, and shifting from direct loans to guaranteed loans. During the 1980s, a declining portion of discretionary domestic resources came from budget authority directly appropriated to the spending account. For this reason, data derived from conventional appropriations sources showed much more spending constraint than those produced by Cogan and Muris in their broader examination of accounts.

This discrepancy was partly due to the determination of Congress to show that it was spending less even when it was providing much more than the President wanted. Recourse to offsetting receipts illustrates how Congress can provide more funds while appropriating less. When Congress directs agencies to shift from direct funding to offsetting fees (as it has for the Patent Office, the Nuclear Regulatory Commission, and other federal agencies), these fees reduce, dollar for dollar, the amount that Congress appropriates and the amount recorded as outlays.

Nonconventional financing arrangements are not new, but they flourish when the budget is tight and the President and Congress clash on spending policy. It must be acknowledged that various nonconventional arrangements may serve the public interest. In many programs, a strong case can be made that costs should be recovered through user charges. But the issue here is not the efficiency of these arrangements but their use to understate available resources. This problem can be corrected by devising accounting formats that reveal the total flow of resources into and out of accounts.

The Arithmetic of Microbudgeting

Once it is recognized that microbudgeting is often the practice of providing more under the guise of cutting the budget, it becomes necessary to probe into the way budgetary actions are scored and reported. The task is not easy, for as microbudgeting expert Roy Meyers argues, there are "two types of budgetary outcomes—'reported outcomes' and 'real outcomes.' Reported outcomes are highly visible, being formally recognized as priorities by budgetary decision processes. These outcomes are appropriations . . . budget authority and outlays. In contrast, real outcomes may not be visible at all."[13] Meyers was moved to distinguish between real and reported outcomes by closely examining one account—the Rural Housing Insurance Fund. Over a twenty-year period (1966–85), this account accumulated $48 billion in program obligations but reported only $16 billion budget authority, $11 billion in outlays, and $8 billion in appropriations. The marked differences between the amounts appropriated and the program levels derived from questionable bookkeeping practices. While this is a truly egregious case, it illustrates how much can be hidden by creative microbudgeting.

It also indicates the difficult task facing microbudgeters who know too much to take official data at face value but often know too little to produce their own numbers. In many cases, nothing less than a detailed reconstruction of the relevant accounts will suffice. What is usually required is a flow analysis that traces funds as they move between accounts, or between the budget and off-budget entities, between direct appropriations and other resources, between new money and reprogrammed old funds, and so on. Of course, not every account has such complex flows as these, but enough do to call official data into question.

The understatement or concealment of expenditures often entails the substitution of one type of resource for another or the substitution of one source of funds for others. These methods tend to be account- or program-specific; that is, they exploit characteristics of the affected accounts but cannot be applied across the board. For example, the sale of "loan assets" to an off-budget agency can only be made by an account that makes direct loans. But at least one widely used device can be applied to virtually all budget accounts: baseline assumptions can be manipulated to affect perceptions of what is happening to the budget. As Timothy Muris shows in Chapter 3, baseline assumptions can be used to score a spending increase as a budget cutback. Although the concept of baselines was introduced as a by-product of the new congressional budget process in the 1970s, it was only in the 1980s that it gained acceptance in both the executive and legislative branches as the measure of spending cuts, revenue changes, and deficit reductions.

The beginning of understanding about the baseline is that it is always an assumed number. This is a radical departure from traditional budget scorekeeping, which is derived from actual numbers, such as the amount appropriated for the previous year or the amount requested by the President. Although aggregated baseline data are published, detailed account-by-account data and assumptions are not. Moreover, it is increasingly the practice to score budgetary actions solely in terms of the baseline. CBO budget documents often display neither the previous (or current) year's figures nor the amounts requested by the President. Similarly, the deficit-reduction projections issued pursuant to budget summit negotiations in 1990 and earlier were computed in terms of unpublished baseline assumptions.

This practice distorts budget perceptions and opens the door to the types of abuses described in Muris's revealing study. Baselines are inherently misleading because they substitute assumed deficit reductions for actual reductions and because they permit politicians to label spending increases as spending cuts. Baselines have legitimate technical uses, such as estimating the effects of inflation or increased participation rates on expenditures. But in the hands of politicians, baselines are much more than technical estimates. They are means by which spending more can be recorded as spending less. It is highly probable that baselines have affected spending trends and have complicated the task of controlling the deficit.

Perhaps the best example of how baselines have affected budgetary perceptions and outcomes is Medicare, a program whose complicated and often questionable baseline assumptions Muris analyzes in Chapter 3. According to official statistics, Medicare was trimmed by more than $50 billion during the 1980s, but its expenditures tripled during the decade from about $35 billion to more than $100 billion a year. While Medicare is an exceptional case, it is far from the only one whose spending pattern has been affected by baseline practices.

A Research Agenda for Microbudgeting

Microbudgeting is hard to study. One cannot rely on reported data, and the real data usually are buried under layers of unpublished assumptions and hard-to-ferret-out financial flows. The task of measuring the full resources available in each account has been eased by a restructuring of the program and financing schedules published in the President's budget. Prior to the fiscal 1992 budget, these schedules—one is prepared for each appropriation account—focused on the new budget authority requested for the fiscal year. Drawing on nonappropriated sources made it easy to lower the appropriation request. The new format shows the gross and net budget authority for each account.

Thus far, the bulk of microbudgeting research has been conducted by former insiders who either have access to detailed data or have learned by experience how to interpret and reconstruct the published records, or by journalists who have gathered anecdotal data to illustrate their stories of how the process operates. The best journalistic accounts of microbudgeting behavior are the long series of articles on the appropriations process published by Dan Morgan in the *Washington Post.*[14] Morgan was released from other assignments for a two-year period during which he filed dozens of revealing stories on the inner workings of the House and Senate appropriations committees. The insider literature includes the chapters in this book by Muris and Cogan and a forthcoming book by Roy Meyers.[15]

Microbudgeting should not be regarded as inaccessible by academic researchers. Questioning and reconstructing the official accounts, digging for data, and explicating the conceptual relationship between institutional behavior and budget outcomes are tasks that can be performed by trained researchers. My view is that the biggest payoff will come from research on the internal budgetary operations of federal agencies. Compared to what happens in federal agencies, budgeting in Congress is an open book. Much more is known about the budgetary actions of committees and members than about the behavior of agency spenders. Much more is known about how agencies put together their budgets than about how they implement them. Very little is known about how money is moved around during the year in response to uncertainties, new pressures, or other factors. It is an observed fact that agencies rarely lay off regular staff, even when they receive a smaller appropriation than they request or funds are impounded or sequestered during the year. We assume that agencies value stability in budgeting and that they protect themselves against uncertainty and exogenous shocks by hoarding money. A microbudgeting study of hoarding would have to investigate an agency's fund structure, the flow of money between funds, reprogramming and other adjustments, and deviations between the requested budget and the actual pattern of expenditure. Getting information on these practices would require a great deal of digging, but researchers can find useful clues in apportionment and allotment schedules, agency work plans and internal budgets, the detailed justification material submitted to the appropriations committees, formal reprogramming requests, transactions in management funds and other revolving funds, and so on.

While the study of Congress is somewhat more advanced, much remains to be uncovered about the actions of the appropriations and authorization committees. Is there a link between the overwhelming support for appropriations bills and the project money distributed in them? We need a fuller accounting of the relationship between these committees and the agencies they oversee. One suspects that the relationship is often much more accommodating than the tensions in formal appropriations hearings would lead one to suspect. It would be useful to catalog the means by which the appropriations committees spend money while cutting the budget.

These are but a small sample of the fertile areas of research warranting attention. Regardless of the subjects selected for inquiry, it is important that the research not be based on aggregated data taken at face value. An essential feature of microbudgeting research must be to reconstruct financial data from the bottom up. Once this work has been done, it should be possible to take a fresh look at the macrobudgeting questions that have been misanswered or not even asked.

APPENDIXES

APPENDIX A

Data Description

The first step in creating the distribution of general-fund program outlays by congressional committees for 1992 is to divide total budget outlays into general-fund and trust-fund expenditures. For 1932, since none of the funds classified as trust funds in this study were in existence, this first step is unnecessary. The source for information on these funds for 1992 is the 1994 *Budget of the U.S. Government*, fiscal year 1994.

General-fund outlays are defined as total budget outlays, excluding federal employer payments for retirement, interest payments to trust funds, and undistributed royalties, less outlays to the public by the six tax-financed trust funds.

The second step was to separate general-fund outlays, program by program, into discretionary programs and mandatory programs. This decomposition was based on the provisions of the 1990 *Budget Enforcement Act*, Public Law PL101-508.

The third step was to assign each so-called mandatory-spending program to the congressional committee having jurisdiction over that program.

Two sources of information were used to make these assignments. The first is a periodic report on the activities of each House and Senate committee made in compliance with the Legislative Reorganization Act of 1946 as amended. These reports are prepared by the individual committees and are submitted to each committee's chamber. Included in each report is a statement of the committee's jurisdiction. These reports are listed in the Bibliography. Another source that was particularly helpful was a 1978 publication by the General Accounting Office, *Table of Federal Programs, March 1977*. This report identifies the jurisdiction of all programs in the budget in 1978.

Once mandatory spending programs (budget accounts) were linked to the relevant committee of jurisdiction, outlays from each account were assigned to its respective committee. Where jurisdiction for a program, such as Medicare Part B, is shared between two committees, the outlays were divided evenly between the two.

TABLE A.1

Distribution of Program Outlays by House Committee, 1992

(as percent of total)

House committee	Total expenditures
Appropriations	41.4%
Ways and Means	41.7
Energy and Commerce	7.5
Agriculture	3.7
Post Office and Civil Service	2.9
Veterans' Affairs	1.6
All other (11 committees)	1.2

Programs (budget accounts) funded by discretionary appropriations were assigned to the Appropriations Committee. No subdivision of the committee into subcommittees was made.

Table 2.2 in the text showed the distribution of general-fund outlays by committee. For completeness, the Table A.1 in this appendix provides the distribution of general-fund outlays by committee.

APPENDIX B

Baseline Concepts

The Congressional Budget Act of 1974

During the debate leading to creation of a centralized congressional budget process, concern over the base to evaluate budget proposals arose. A major problem was that many in Congress felt themselves ignorant of where government spending was headed. They desired a tool prepared by experts for improving decision making, one that would forecast future trends and provide an objective, policy-neutral method to measure the potential impact of proposed changes.[1] At hearings in 1973,[2] recalling his experience as governor of Maine, noting that his state used this budget for evaluating proposed program changes, Senator Muskie claimed that such a baseline was needed to tell Congress and the people "what it would cost to do what the government was currently doing."[3]

Four months later, Muskie proposed to require the President to submit "the estimated expenditures and proposed appropriations . . . for the ensuing year if all programs and activities were carried on . . . at the same level as the fiscal year in progress and without policy changes in such programs and activities."[4] This proposal became law and continues in effect today. As recodified to its current form, the definition reads: "the estimated budget outlays and proposed budget authority that would be included in the budget for the following fiscal year if programs and activities of the United States government were carried on during the year at the same level as the current fiscal year without a change in policy."[5]

The sparse legislative history supports Senator Muskie's purpose. As Senator Ervin, sponsor of the entire bill, stated in floor debate, the baseline would serve "the purpose of acquainting Congress with what costs would be if existing programs were to be extended for another year without change," thereby giving "Congress information about the expenditures of the programs that are in existence during the preceding year and what they would be if continued unchanged during the next fiscal year so that we have that to compare to the new requests in the President's budget that comes down later."[6] Experts would compile an objective baseline that would facilitate better congressional decision making.

How to Define the Baseline

The Budget Act itself is inconclusive. One issue arises from ambiguity in the precise meaning of the words of the act, which require the baseline to measure the amount necessary "if programs and activities . . . were carried on during the year at the same level as the current fiscal year without a change in policy." One meaning of those words, as expressed in the preceding quotes from Senators Muskie and Ervin, is to measure a constant level of government, allowing one to see if a proposed change in spending would increase or decrease government. This is "current services," a measure of what it would cost in the future to provide the services the government provides today. Others read the statute differently, focusing on the words "without a change in policy." Under this view, the baseline should put the government on "automatic pilot" and determine how much it would cost to fund it in the future.[7] This view is "current policy."[8]

Although many believe that current policy provides a good proxy for current services, these two definitions produce different results. Consider, for example, entitlements, programs for which Congress decides basic eligibility criteria, leaving the government obligated to pay the legislated amount for all who are "entitled." Government expenditures for these programs depend not on an annual vote of Congress but upon the definitions of the original statute and the number of people who claim benefits. As the number of entitled beneficiaries increases, outlays inexorably grow. For example, outlays for the largest entitlement, Social Security, grow each year as the population ages. Moreover, many programs, including Social Security, are automatically indexed for inflation, with recipients receiving an annual cost of living adjustment (COLA). Including adjustments for COLAs and new beneficiaries as part of current services, the procedure adopted, significantly increases the baseline compared to using the previous year as the base. For example, the Social Security baseline of the Congressional Budget Office (CBO) grew from $315 billion in 1990 to $340 billion in 1991.*

**See* U.S. Congress, CBO, *Economic and Budget Outlook: 1990–1995*, 1990. Most of the increase resulted from an increase in the number of eligible recipients and the costs of the COLA. A third cause of increase is that those newly eligible recipients who simply replace deceased recipients receive higher average benefits. The OMB as well as the CBO prepares a baseline. The two baselines will differ primarily because of different use of economic assumptions (for example, OMB had

If the question is how much does it cost next year to provide this year's government, then the increase in program eligibility should be included in the base to avoid reducing individual benefits. The case for including the cost of living increase is arguably more tentative, depending on one's view of what level of services are "current," but the decision to include COLAs is defended as necessary to keep the purchasing power of recipients at current levels and because the COLA is in current law.

More controversial issues exist, however. One involves Congress increasing benefit levels but phasing them in over time. For example, the increase might pass in 1989, with little impact in 1989 and full implementation delayed until 1994. When 1994 arrives, are these new benefits in the baseline or are they increases to it? Current services, as defined here, would treat the expansion as occurring in 1994 when it was actually implemented. Only in 1994 does government actually grow. Current policy, on the other hand, would say that no expansion occurs in 1994 because the law was passed previously, making the expansion "in the baseline" for 1994. Current policy thus treats as current all laws as they exist, even if they call for large changes from current services in the future.

A similar issue involves expiring provisions of law. Congressional pay policy provides an example. The permanent date for pay increases to be effective was October 1, the first day of the fiscal year. For much of the 1980s, Congress annually delayed the effective date to January 1. Because this change was made one year at a time, any pay increase in the next year was legally effective on October 1. When Congress extended its practice of beginning increases on January 1, under current services there would have been no "savings" from the delay because the congressional practice had been to pay on January 1. Under current policy, however, "savings" were counted because regardless of past practice, the law existing at the time of the delay to January 1 required the pay raise to begin on October 1. This difference between how current services and current policy treat phased-in changes and expiring provisions is summarized in Table B.1. The current services definition excludes such manipulations when calculating the baseline; current policy includes them. (Current law will be discussed below.)

Another controversial issue involves discretionary programs. In contrast to entitlements, discretionary programs, such as the defense budget and funding for regulatory agencies, NASA, IRS, and the Department of Justice are reviewed annually, with Congress voting on next year's level of

a 4.0 percent CPI increase in its 1991 baseline, compared to CBO's 4.3 percent), "technical" differences (for example, OMB and CBO may disagree on the number of participants who will become newly eligible), and conceptual differences (for example, differences in how current services should be defined for a particular program).

TABLE B.1
Baseline Definitions

	Phased-in and expiring changes	Discretionary inflation	Mandatory inflation
Current Services	Excluded	Included if necessary to fund current program	Included at level necessary to provide current level of service
Current Policy	Included	Included at uniform levels	Included at levels based on past program performance, even if growth exceeds general inflation
Current Law	Included	Excluded	Included if required by law

new budgetary resources.* Because these programs do not automatically grow as entitlements do, the question becomes whether the baseline should inflate them above last year's level and if so, by what amount. Current policy uses a mechanical formula to inflate these programs. It does not ask case by case how much is actually needed to continue a program at current levels. Current services is more complicated; it would include inflation if necessary to fund the program currently approved by Congress, a point considered in detail in Chapter 3. As discussed there, the decision of how to inflate discretionary programs if at all can be made only by evaluating programs individually.

Table B.1 summarizes the difference between current services and current policy regarding discretionary programs. Although current policy inflates these programs, inflation for discretionary programs is not necessary to measure the cost of a government on automatic pilot. There is *no* automatic pilot for discretionary programs. Decisions are made annually, and new funds are not provided without a new law. Nevertheless, proponents of current policy often defend their inflation decision as measuring current services—that is, as providing a constant level of government.[9]

The decision to inflate discretionaries was controversial in the 1970s. Many who accepted the automatic pilot concept of the baseline rejected an inflation adjustment. They argued that the proper definition of automatic

*Congress appropriates authority to spend, not outlays. Outlays occur when money is actually disbursed from the Treasury. For construction programs, such as the building of ships, the authority may not outlay until years after it is appropriated. For other programs, like salaries for government employees, outlays occur in the year authority is appropriated. Chapter 4 discusses funding sources for discretionary programs in detail.

pilot would assume that discretionary programs continued at the level Congress last approved. This baseline is "current law." Current law differs from current policy for discretionary programs but follows current policy for phased-in programs and expiring provisions.*

Inflation for entitlements presents a third issue, one on which each baseline gives a different answer. Some programs grow much faster than the general level of inflation. Moreover, decisions regarding inflation for some mandatory programs, such as Medicare, have often been made annually, either by Congress or by regulatory agencies. (Strictly speaking, such decisions should be called discretionary, although this is not the common practice.) The amount the baseline should inflate such programs, if at all, is in dispute. Current policy provides the inflation necessary to fund the program, whether or not that inflation is required by law or is a large or small increase. Current law inflates entitlements to the extent required by law. Current services inflates mandatories, but the appropriate inflation increase can differ among programs and between current services and the existing definition of current policy. Table B.1 summarizes these differences.

*Most definitions of current law would include phase-ins because they are included in the law that currently exists; others exclude them because they are not in the law currently enforced. In any event, the inflation issue was the distinction most frequently mentioned between current law and current policy when the choice of baselines was debated in the late 1970s.

REFERENCE MATTER

Notes

Chapter 1

1. Schick, *Congress and Money*, chap. 2, "The Seven-Year Budget War."

2. U.S. OMB, *Budget*, FY 1992, *Historical Tables*, Table 8.1.

3. The Budget Enforcement Act of 1990 is Title XIII of the Omnibus Budget Reconciliation Act of 1990, PL101-508. Its provisions are explained in Keith and Davis, *Budget Enforcement Act of 1990*.

4. The elasticity of the new deficit rules became apparent within months after they were devised. In July 1991, the White House issued its midsession review of the budget. This review, undertaken barely five months after the original budget for fiscal year 1992 had been published, raised that year's estimated deficit by $67 billion. The soaring deficit did not trigger a sequester, nor did it violate the 1990 Budget Enforcement Act; it simply floated upward, as allowed by law, for various "uncontrollable" reasons.

5. Using OMB files, these researchers found that during the course of preparing the budget, OMB often traded off higher budget authority for lower outlays. Compared to the targets set at the start of the preparation process, the budget submitted to Congress generally had more budget authority and lower estimated outlays. Kamlet, "Budgetary Side Payments"; also Kamlet and Mowery, "Presidential Management."

6. Participation certificates (PCs) are pools of government loans that are sold to financial institutions. The revenue from these sales are budgeted as offsetting receipts. They reduce both total outlays and the size of the deficit. The volume of PCs outstanding increased tenfold, from $1.2 billion in 1964 to about $12 billion in 1968. See "Loans, Participation Certificates, and the Financing of Budget Deficits," in President's Commission, *Staff Papers*, pp. 279–300.

7. When it was established, the Federal Financing Bank was an off-budget entity authorized to purchase any obligation guaranteed in whole or in part by a federal agency. The effect of these purchases was to remove various transactions from the budget. See U.S. Congress, Committee on the Budget, House, *Congressional Control*, esp. pp. 78–79, 91.

8. The most immediate effect of the unified budget was to reduce the stated deficit by allowing surpluses in trust funds to offset deficits in the rest of the budget.

9. The theme of this and the next two paragraphs is elaborated in Schick, *Capacity to Budget*, pp. 51–83.

10. The highest official rate set in the 1986 act was 28 percent, but because of the phasing out of certain preferences, many taxpayers had an effective marginal tax rate of 33 percent.

11. The reorientation of OMB is discussed in two articles by Bruce Johnston: "OMB and the Budget Examiner" and "OMB Examiner."

12. The impact of David Stockman on OMB is discussed in Heclo, "Executive Budget Making."

13. An SAP is a letter sent by the Director of OMB to party leaders on each appropriations bill as it moves through Congress. An SAP is normally transmitted in response to subcommittee action, Appropriations Committee markup, and floor action in each chamber. Thus, there will typically be six or more SAPs for each appropriations bill. The SAP informs Congress of objectionable items that might trigger a veto recommendation.

14. Section 302 of the 1974 Budget Act and Section 602 of the 1990 Budget Enforcement Act provide for the budget committees to allocate the budget authority and outlays set forth in a budget resolution among House and Senate committees with direct spending jurisdiction. The Senate allocations are made in one lump sum to each committee; the House Budget Committee, however, breaks down its allocations by functional categories. These functional allocations are frequently ignored by the appropriations committees.

15. House and Senate voting patterns on congressional budget resolutions are recorded in Ornstein et al., tables 7-1 and 7-2.

16. The main product of the budget committees is the budget resolution, which is not legislation. The budget committees do report reconciliation bills, but they are barred from making substantive changes in the legislation formulated by the committees of jurisdiction.

17. The original package negotiated by congressional leaders and the White House was rejected; the enacted package was more heavily shaped by congressional committees, though summit negotiators did keep a watchful eye on what the committees did.

Chapter 2

1. I am especially grateful to Mary Farrell for her invaluable assistance in all aspects of this chapter. Matt Hall and Mary Sprague performed many of the computations. I also wish to thank Janine Hodgson for her

expert help in preparing the manuscript. I have benefited from the comments of David Brady, Bruce Bueno de Mesquita, Carl Dahlman, John Ferejohn, Roger Freeman, Keith Krehbiel, Tim Muris, Ron Pavellas, Alvin Rabushka, John Raisian, and Barry Weingast.

2. Demsetz, "Property Rights"; Hardin, "Tragedy of the Commons."

3. U.S. OMB, *Budget*, FY 1992, *Historical Tables*.

4. The definition of *trust funds* used in this paper differs from the official U.S. Budget definition. For the purposes of this study, only six major federally tax-financed trust funds are included as trust funds: Social Security Old-Age and Survivors Insurance, Social Security Disability, Railroad Retirement, Federal Aid to Highways, Medicare Hospital Insurance (Part A), and the Airport and Airways fund. Together, these six funds account for 80 percent of all trust-fund expenditures and 85 percent of all trust-fund receipts (OMB, *Special Analyses*, 1991). The Unemployment Insurance trust fund, which is also tax financed, is excluded from this group because over 90 percent of its revenue is derived from taxes levied by the individual states and thus is outside the control of the Congress. It is also excluded from the general fund budget calculations.

In addition to these tax-financed trust funds, the official U.S. Budget contains over seventy other trust funds. This latter group is financed either wholly or primarily by general-fund revenues. They are of three generic types. One may be thought of as hybrid trust funds, only partially financed by taxes and collections from the public. The other source of funding is general revenues. This first type includes Black Lung Benefits, Civilian and Military Retirement, and Medicare (Part B). A second consists of trust funds financed through gifts and donations. Almost every government cabinet agency and the legislative branch has at least one such trust fund. A final type of trust fund is one financed entirely by general revenues. The General Revenue Sharing Trust Fund (no longer in existence) is an example of this type of fund. For the purposes of this study, these three types of trust funds are treated as general-fund programs.

5. Trust-fund revenues in Figure 2.2 include both taxes collected from the public and intergovernmental transfers, such as interest payments on trust-fund loans to the general fund and military wage credits to the Social Security funds. These intergovernmental transfers account for 10–15 percent of total trust receipts. Similarly, general-fund outlays include intergovernmental transfers to the trust funds. Such transfers constitute only about 5 percent of general outlays.

6. The details of how Table 2.2 is constructed are provided in Appendix A of this book.

7. In computing each committee's share of outlays, interest on the national debt, IRS tax refunds (for 1932), and veterans compensation and

pensions were excluded from total general-fund outlays. The exclusion of veterans payments requires some explanation. In 1932, these veterans payments constituted 20 percent of the entire noninterest budget expenditures and 70 percent of all outlays not under the control of the Appropriations Committee. The large magnitude of the outlays reflects the high lingering costs of World War I. Their relatively large size was only a temporary phenomenon. By 1939, veterans payments had declined to 5 percent of the budget. To include these war-related payments would have distorted the relative importance of spending authority among committees.

8. Schick, *Legislation*. The use of borrowing authority was challenged after World War II. Opponents argued that borrowing authority violated a 1920 House rule that granted to the Appropriations Committee the sole authority to report legislation making appropriations. The challenge was defeated, however, when the House decided that making funds available for obligation by this method did not constitute an appropriation. (U.S. Congress, *Congressional Record*, June 28, 1949, p. 8538.)

9. U.S. OMB, *Budget*, 1953.

10. U.S. OMB, *Budget*, 1964.

11. The World War II years witnessed the widespread adoption of another technique, contract authority, to circumvent the appropriations process. Contract authority authorizes an agency to enter into contracts to undertake a particular project in advance of an appropriation. Thus, as a practical matter, federal funds have already been committed at the time the appropriation is made. The Appropriations Committee action is therefore purely pro forma. To expedite the process of financing the World War II effort, congressional committees made widespread use of this device. For example, to aid in the final push to end the war in the Pacific, 25 percent of all general-fund appropriations were used to liquidate prior contract authorizations (U.S. OMB, *Budget*, 1947).

Following the war, the legislative committees continued to make liberal use of contract authority. Contract authority was used by almost every legislative committee to finance almost every conceivable type of construction activity. In 1951, more than fifty budget accounts were funded through contract authority. These accounts included such activities as Public Health Service grants for hospital construction, various GSA office construction projects, aid to airports, the Alaska Railroad, and construction activities of the Bonneville Power Administration and National Park Service (U.S. OMB, *Budget*, 1953). Despite the large number of accounts, total expenditures funded through this device were relatively small.

12. Glasson, *Federal Military Pensions*; McNeil et al., *Military Retirement*.

13. See Schick, *Congress and Money*, for a comprehensive discussion of the history and impact of the act.

14. The committee reforms in the House that were adopted late in the same year arguably had an important effect of increasing the degree of decentralization over financial matters. Particularly important was the transfer of jurisdiction for general-fund health-care entitlements, Medicaid and Medicare (Part B), from the Ways and Means Committee to the Energy and Commerce Committee (*Congressional Quarterly* 1974, p. 635).

15. The problems of the budget and the forest are instances of what has become known as the "tragedy of the commons," after an article by the same title written two decades ago by Garrett Hardin. The general rule of the tragedy is that open access to a common resource leads to overconsumption and eventual exhaustion of the common resource. In the words of Hardin, "Freedom in a commons brings ruin to all" (Hardin, p. 1244). In the economic literature, the common resource problem is discussed at length by Demsetz, "Property Rights."

16. U.S. Congress, House Report 373.

17. Ibid.

18. The rationale for the change was that because of the increased work load, the job of handling revenues, expenditures, and banking and currency matters was too burdensome for a single committee to handle in a well-considered but expeditious manner. As Representative Samuel Cox remarked during the floor debate, "No set of men, however enduring their patience, studious their habits or gigantic their mental grasp and overburdened with the labor incident to the existing monetary condition of the country growing out of this unparalleled civil strife can do this labor as well as the people have a right to expect" (U.S. Congress, *Congressional Globe*, Mar. 2, 1865, p. 1312).

19. Following a somewhat shaky start during the 1790s, the budget ran surpluses each year through 1835 except during the War of 1812 and three years in the 1820s, two of which were years of severe economic contraction (U.S. Treasury 1980; Dewey, *Financial History*).

20. Dewey, *Financial History.*

21. U.S. Dept. of the Treasury, *Annual Report*, 1980; Dewey, *Financial History.*

22. The Senate transferred appropriations jurisdiction for Rivers and Harbors from the Appropriations Committee to the Senate Committee on Commerce in 1877.

23. The Senate divided jurisdiction in 1899. The resolution to split jurisdiction was taken up under unanimous consent and adopted without any floor debate (*Congressional Record*, Jan. 27, 1899). As a result of the

Senate action, the Senate Appropriations Committee retained responsibility for only three supply bills: the Legislative, Executive and Judicial bill, the Sundry Civil bill, and the deficiency bill. Jurisdiction for the remaining 80 percent of all discretionary appropriations was divided among ten separate legislative committees.

24. Nonmandatory appropriations exclude permanent appropriations such as interest on the national debt and those that are treated as pro forma appropriations, such as Veterans Pensions.

25. U.S. Dept. of the Treasury, *Annual Report*, 1980.

26. Appropriations totals are limited to those for annually funded discretionary programs. Thus, excluded from the appropriations enacted for any given year are permanent appropriations, such as interest on the national debt, and appropriations contained in private relief bills. Appropriations in private relief bills are not under the jurisdiction of the appropriations committees and should be viewed in the modern rubric of budgeting as appropriated entitlements. Also, and most important, veterans pensions are excluded from the totals on the ground that the enabling statutes make these pensions an entitlement.

The growth in pensions during this sixteen-year period and throughout the remainder of the nineteenth century is particularly noteworthy. Expenditures on pensions, after remaining roughly constant throughout the decade of the 1870s, began to soar in 1880. From 1878 to 1886, expenditure on pensions rose by 133 percent. Its growth alone accounts for more than one-half of the entire growth in government noninterest expenditures. The increase is the result of a single law, the Pension Arrears Act of 1879, which provided benefits retroactive to the date of disability to all veterans who were disabled in the line of duty during the Civil War.

27. The 1878 appropriation bill for Rivers and Harbors was the first to bypass the House Appropriations Committee. However, no final appropriation bill was agreed to; hence, FY78 appropriations are excluded from the data.

28. Kremer, p. 128.

29. Hart, p. 93.

30. U.S. Congress, House Report 373.

31. Ibid.

32. Ibid.

33. Ibid.

34. Willoughby, *National Budget System.*

35. *Congressional Record*, June 1, 1920.

36. Willoughby, p. 37.

37. *Congressional Record*, June 1, 1920, p. 8116.

38. As Willoughby notes, the rules governing the House and Senate differ. But the principles underlying them are the same.

39. Wartime expenditures peaked in 1919 at $18.5 billion. Outlays then declined to $6.4 billion in 1920, to $5.1 billion in 1921, to $3.3 billion in 1922.

40. For purposes of comparison, the general-fund budget has been in deficit thirty-five years since 1950. The longest string of consecutive deficits is the current one, twenty-seven years.

41. The Railroad Retirement fund has been financially insolvent for most of the post–World War II period. In the early 1950s, the fund required a sizable infusion of revenues from the Social Security trust fund, and since the mid-1970s, the fund has received an annual "windfall subsidy" from the general fund. Despite these bailouts, benefit payments continually exceed receipts; as a consequence, annual loans from the general fund are required. The fiscal problem faced by the fund is in part due to the employment problems in the railroad industry. A combination of forces has produced an almost perpetual decline in rail employment since the early 1960s. Since revenues for the trust fund are derived from a payroll tax, the fund faces a chronic insufficiency of revenues. The secular employment decline has affected the trust fund much as a long-term aggregate economic decline would affect the solvency of any of the other tax-financed trust funds.

42. Derthick, *Policymaking*.

43. In the case of the highway trust fund, a similar situation arose (Schwartz, *Urban Freeways*). The basic objective of the program was to complete the interstate highway system. The expected time it would take to complete the job and the dollar cost of the program were known (or thought to be). One available financing option was a gasoline tax that would be set to finance the program on a pay-as-you-go basis. Another option was to finance the entire present and future costs of completing the highway system at the start of the program by issuing government bonds to the public. They chose the former.

Chapter 3

The author gratefully acknowledges the financial support of the Smith-Richardson Foundation, through a grant to the Hoover Institution, and the assistance of the staff of OMB, especially the Budget Review and Health and Income Maintenance divisions, without whose instruction, patience, and skill this chapter could not have been written. I have benefited from the comments of John Cogan, Hugh Connally, Carol Cox, Ed Dale, Jeff Sanders, Allen Schick, Art Stigile, and Barry Weingast.

1. See U.S. Congress, CBO, *Economic and Budget Outlook: Fiscal Years 1992–1996*, p. 152.

2. Ibid., p. 91.

3. Congressional Budget and Impoundment Control Act of 1974, Title VI, Sec. 605 (PL 93-344, 88 Stat. 297, 1974).

4. See, e.g., U.S. Congress, Joint Economic Committee, "1975 Budget" and "1976 Current Services Budget."

5. For definitions similar to those used in this chapter, see *Congressional Quarterly*, "Federal Budget Process," and Wildavsky, *New Politics*.

6. Letter from David G. Mathiasen, Deputy Asst. Director for Budget Review, OMB, to Frederick B. Wolf, Director, Accounting and Financial Management Division, GAO, reprinted in GAO, *President's Current Services Budget*.

7. For a discussion of the Senate's use of baselines in the 1970s, see Schick, *Congress and Money*, pp. 261–64.

8. Reagan Administration, Mar. 1981, p. 139; see also Feb. 1981.

9. Kenneth Bacon, "Reagan Urges Speedy Action on Tax and Budget Cuts to Combat 'Economic Stagnation' and High Inflation," *Wall Street Journal*, Mar. 11, 1981, p. 3; John M. Berry and Leo Lescarze, "Reagan Sends Budget to Hill as 'Mandate for Change,'" *Washington Post*, Mar. 11, 1981, p. 1; Edward Cowan, "Reagan Delivers His Budget to Congress with a Warning to Remember 'Our Mandate,'" *New York Times*, Mar. 11, 1981, p. 1; Albert R. Hunt, "Reagan's Budget Aide Shaped Economic Plan with Firmness, Skill," *Wall Street Journal*, Feb. 19, 1981, p. 1; Leo Lescarze and Lou Cannon, "Reagan to Hill: 'People Are Waiting,'" *Washington Post*, Feb. 19, 1981, p. 1; "President Formally Submits Cuts in Fiscal 1982 Budget to Congress," *Wall Street Journal*, Mar. 11, 1981, pp. 2–5; Steven R. Weisman, "President Proposes 83 Major Program Cuts; Tells Congress U.S. Faces 'Day of Reckoning,'" *New York Times*, Feb. 19, 1981, p. 1.

10. Weisman, "President Proposes." Other stories gave more emphasis to absolute numbers, although the "cut" concept still figured prominently. For example, the *Times* story of March 11 ran the year-to-year changes on the front page.

11. See Table 3.1 (the author participated in the negotiations).

12. OMB has published "Current Services Estimates" in its budgets, except for fiscal 1991, when the term was not used.

13. U.S. Dept. of Labor, *Budget Justifications*. Of course, if the program's purpose would have required more money per person to accomplish, current services should not consider this addition an increase.

14. See U.S. Congress, CBO, *NASA Program*.

15. See U.S. Congress, CBO, *Operations and Support Costs*.

16. Mathiasen letter cited in note 6.

17. Executive Office of the President, OMB, *Budget of the United States Government*, FY *1992*, pp. 4–202. There were about 2.1 million active-duty military forces in 1990. Total executive branch civilian employment was estimated at 3.0 million, including 1 million civilians in defense military functions. Ibid., p. 201. Average costs per employee vary, but $40,000–$50,000 is frequently used.

18. Executive Office of the President, OMB, *Budget of the United States Government Fiscal Year 1977*, appendix, p. 829; *Budget of the United States Government FY 1987*, p. 1L-5; U.S. Dept. of Commerce, Bureau of the Census, *Statistical Abstract of the United States, 1979*, p. 336; *Statistical Abstract of the United States, 1988*, p. 343.

19. One can obtain the flavor of these debates from the 1990 Defense Appropriations and Authorization hearings in the Senate (Sept. 19) and the House (Feb. 5–8).

20. For example, "Blue Chip Economic Indicators," published by Capitol Publications.

21. U.S. Congress, CBO, *Economic and Budget Outlook: Fiscal Years 1992–1996*, p. 150.

22. U.S. Congress, CBO, *Pay-As-You-Go Budgeting.*

23. E.g., Davis, "Cost Containment."

24. See U.S. Congress, HR, Committee on Ways and Means, *Background Materials* (1990), p. 137.

25. U.S. Code, Title 42, Sec. 1395 ww(e)(2) and (3). In the absence of a decision to increase payments, past payments would not have increased automatically.

26. GAO, *Medicare Past Overuse*, Mar. 1986; Kusserow 1987. Hospital margins have recently decreased, and some hospitals are in financial trouble, particularly those in rural areas with many empty beds. Average hospital margins, however, were still relatively high through the 1980s. Most hospitals are nonprofit and thus are not supposed to "profit" from Medicare. For claims of hospitals and the opposing views of many economists, see Rich 1988.

27. U.S. Congress, CBO, *Physician Reimbursement*, pp. xvii–xix.

28. Mowery, pp. 608–10.

29. Executive Office of the President, OMB, *Budget of the United States Government*, FY 1989, *Historical Tables*, pp. 1.1(1)–1.2(2).

30. U.S. Congress, CBO, *The Economic and Budget Outlook: FY 1986–90*, App. D. Politicians frequently note the massive deficit reduction they have enacted. See, e.g., Senator Moynihan's statement during the National Economic Commission hearing of May 10, 1988.

31. Executive Office of the President, OMB, *Special Analysis.*

32. The figure for 1990 was obtained from the OMB *Mid-Season Review.* Figures for 1991 and 1992 were obtained from OMB estimates at the time of the summit.

33. For a critique of press coverage see Bethel, "Smoke, Mirrors," detailing the lack of coverage of overall figures in the *Wall Street Journal, New York Times*, and *Washington Post*, and discussing how the *Wall Street Journal* defended this lack by claiming that "the outlay figures do not capture the controversy and the choices being made." Ibid., p. 15.

34. Only $4.4 billion in cuts was achieved from the administration's baseline because of the difference in defining Medicare current policy.

35. To avoid the impact of technical re-estimates, which necessarily cause minor uncertainty, the $35 billion is measured against Medicare estimates as of Jan. 1991. Following CBO practice, unless otherwise indicated changes in the Medicare Part B premium are not scored as a reduction in the Medicare program. Table 3.1, however, was expressly prepared at the 1987 summit and includes the Part B premium extension as a Medicare reduction.

36. See Executive Office of the President, OMB, *Budget of the United States Government, FY 1989*, chap. 4. Social Security payroll taxes are the source of the additional new receipts. Because the Social Security system is running a surplus, these taxes will be invested in government securities, thereby reducing the deficit and causing other programs to feel less pressure for budget restraint.

37. See Hoagland, "Omnibus Budget Reconciliation Act."

38. See *Background Materials*, cited in n. 24, and HHS estimates provided to the author.

39. The derivation of these numbers is explained in the next section of this paper. As discussed there, the $7 billion does not include reductions obtained from extending the recent Medicare policy of PPS updates below the market basket.

40. HHS estimated the "savings" to be $8.2 billion.

41. HHS estimated the "savings" to be $4.9 billion.

42. $1.9 billion of savings over three years resulted from 50 percent absorption of the increase by the agencies whose employees received it (the baseline assumed none). U.S. Congress, CBO, *Budgetary Treatment.* In 1990, pay policy changed to become more consistent with private sector changes, eliminating, for the time being, such manipulation. See "Congress Out to Cut Pay Gap," *Congressional Quarterly* 48, Aug. 25, 1990, p. 2710. The policy is aimed at increasing wages up to 5 percent annually over the five years, closing the average 30 percent gap behind private sector workers.

43. See GAO, *U.S.D.A.'s Commodity Program.*

44. This statistic was compiled by comparing the estimate in the budget for each fiscal year with the actual required expenditure.

45. U.S. Dept. of Health and Human Services, *Justification of Budget.* The statistics that follow regarding "cuts" were compiled by analysis from CBO and HHS estimates. Moreover, these numbers are an approximation, because they simply add projections made at or near the time of passage of provisions enacted in different years. The estimates thus use different economic and technical assumptions, and provisions passed in subsequent years may in fact interact with provisions passed earlier, thereby changing the estimates if they were recalculated.

46. Also relevant is the experience with the physician "freeze," in which spending grew despite the freeze.

47. GAO, *Medicare Laboratory Fee Schedules*, pp. 22–23.

48. This paragraph is based on conversations with OMB and HHS analysts.

49. See Haas, "When a Cut Is Not All That Unkind" (also discussing the problem of double-counting of savings).

50. See *Background Materials* cited in note 24, p. 837.

51. See Hoagland, "Omnibus Budget Reconciliation Act." CBO's January report listed $16.7 billion as increased outlays from the EITC provision.

52. Hoagland, p. 11.

53. Much of the pre-1980s literature on budgeting focused on using the previous year as a base, and on the increment added in the next budget year. See, e.g., Wildavsky, *Politics*, 1964 ed; Kamlet and Mowery, "Budgetary Base."

54. U.S. Congress, CBO, *Profile*, pp. 32–33.

55. See Wildavsky, *New Politics*, pp. 202–3.

56. This $54 billion was compiled by analysis from CBO and HHS estimates. The universe of "cuts" were reprinted in U.S. Congress, HR, Committee on Ways and Means, *Background Material*, 1987, pp. 168–70; updated to include the 1987 budget summit. Table 3.2 provides estimates for the 1990 budget summit. The decision whether cuts were "hard" or "soft," as explained in the next paragraph of the text, was based on discussions with administration officials.

57. See, e.g., Feder, Hadley, and Zuckerman, "Medicare's Hospital Prospective Payment System."

58. The premium extension is included as a Medicare reduction in this calculation.

59. See, e.g., Becker, *Economic Approach*; Buchanan and Tullock, *Calculus of Consent*; McCormick and Tollison, *Politicians*.

60. Robert Pear, "Reagan's Budget Asking Cutbacks in Health Plans, Increases in Military," *New York Times*, Feb. 4, 1986, p. A-1.

61. Rich, "Reagan to Propose Substantial Increase for Defense, Space," *Washington Post*, Feb. 3, 1986, p. A-1.

62. See, e.g., "The Budget Poll," *Washington Post* editorial of Feb. 15, 1986. See also *Business Week*, Aug. 22, 1988, p. 34 (quoting experts that restraining the rate of growth of federal outlays to 4 percent a year would require large "cuts"); Lawrence Haas, "Budget Focus—Genuine Cut," *National Journal*, Aug. 15, 1987, p. 2124 (noting manipulation of current policy); Yang, "Waxman Spearheads Congress' Counterattack Against Reagan Effort to Cut Back Health Care," *Wall Street Journal*, p. A-12 (Oct. 12, 1988).

63. See, e.g., Taylor, "Most Americans Oppose Reagan Budget Priorities," *Washington Post*, Feb. 14, 1986, p. A-4.

Chapter 4

Technical assistance was provided by Carey P. Modlin, formerly Assistant Director for Budget Review, U.S. Office of Management and Budget. The authors gratefully acknowledge the financial support provided by grants from the Bradley Foundation and the Smith-Richardson Foundation to the Hoover Institution. We also thank Steve Gunn, Janine Hodgson, Erik Johnson, Sai Prakash, Tim Trujillo, and Nicole Verrier for their research assistance. Helpful comments were received from Stan Collender, Dan Crippen, Edwin Dale, Arlene Holen, Rudy Penner, Allen Schick, and Joseph Wright.

1. Paul Bluestein and Alan Murray, "Reagan, Congress Gird For Fight Over Need to Meet Deficit Target," *Wall Street Journal*, Jan. 5, 1987, p. 10. Examples of other statements in Congressional Committee and members reports include U.S. Congress, Committee on the Budget, Senate, *President's 1989 Budget*, pp. 49–50 ("The Reagan legacy in domestic discretionary spending is a bitter one.... The Reagan legacy in defense spending is one of unprecedented peacetime growth"); Dan Morgan, "College of Cardinals, A Summer of Frustration," *Washington Post*, June 30, 1989, p. A-14 (the appropriators "are like members of an old monied family that has fallen on hard times and is living in reduced circumstances"); U.S. Senate, Committee on the Budget, *Framework for the 1990 Budget Resolution*, p. 6 ("Over the last eight years domestic discretionary spending has borne the brunt of deficit reduction").

2. Summary statements of this view include: U.S. Senate, Committee on the Budget, *Framework for the 1990 Budget Resolution*, p. 6 (the decrease

in domestic discretionary spending "translates to an under investment in many areas, including a serious drop in the federal commitment to education and an inability to meet the research and development demands that will take us into the twenty-first century"); *Los Angeles Times*, Oct. 8, 1988 ("the [homeless] problem has reached crisis proportions for two reasons. First, the federal housing budget has been decimated, cut by 78 percent since President Reagan took office in 1981").

3. In official federal budget jargon, nonentitlement domestic spending is termed "domestic discretionary" spending. Also, throughout this chapter the data are often adjusted for inflation. To make this adjustment we use the composite Gross National Product Deflator (U.S. OMB, *Budget*, 1991, table 1.3).

4. These reductions are described later in this chapter.

5. U.S. Congress, CBO, *Economic and Budget Outlook: FY 1991–1995*, table E-5, p. 126.

6. Money the government collects from the public is classified either as governmental receipts, which are the amounts compared to outlays for calculating the budget deficit, or offsetting collections, which are amounts deducted from disbursements in calculating outlays. See Cuny, "Offsetting Collections."

7. The appropriations committees use budget authority as the primary measure of their allocations to discretionary programs.

8. Appropriated budget authority for the highway trust fund is liquidating authority—the authority to liquidate or pay prior obligations—and has no control function.

9. Despite this equality, during the 1980s Congress did not add obligation limitations to appropriated budget authority in determining budget allocations in congressional budget resolutions.

10. Because all the budget authority obligated in a year is not liquidated (paid) in the same year, outlays for 1981 (for example) do not equal budget authority. For simplicity, a recovery of $5 million in prior-year obligations in 1989 is ignored. This recovery increased budgetary resources that year to $206 million.

11. PL 96-517.

12. PL 97-247.

13. One should not conclude that it is inappropriate to net offsetting receipts against expenditures in all cases. Especially in the case of public enterprise funds, in which collections from the public are used to finance an ongoing cycle of business type operations, netting collections against expenditures is not only legitimate but informative. Under this convention, any shortfall of receipts relative to expenditures that is met through general taxpayer funds is immediately highlighted. A more complete treat-

ment of this issue can be found in the *Report of the President's Commission on Budget Concepts, 1967.*

14. This practice continues to become more prevalent in the 1990s.

15. See Executive Office, OMB, *Budget of the United States Government, FY 1991.* Besides antitrust, the FTC spends resources on consumer protection and economic reports. The numbers in the text thus overstate federal antitrust totals. The FTC spent about half of its $66 million in 1989 on antitrust activities.

16. U.S. Congress, HR, Committee on Appropriations, *Hearings*, p. 95.

17. Because the full amount of support to which farmers are entitled is paid regardless of the amount transferred to the ASCS, the funds transferred are not offset by a decrease in entitlement spending. Thus, total federal spending increases.

18. See *Congressional Quarterly*, "Increase in FHA Mortgage Cap." According to the article, one major reason for the increase in the cap was to raise revenues that the appropriators could spend elsewhere while still allowing sufficient funds for department operation.

19. Other notable examples of programs that have been increasingly financed through the use of receipts from the public rather than the appropriation of budget authority include the operations of the International Trade Administration and the Indian Health Service, salaries and expenses of the Farm Credit Administration, the administration of the Bureau of Printing and Engraving, salaries of the Bureau of the Mint, and the Immigration and Naturalization Service's operations.

20. Most transfers from entitlement to discretionary programs are for the purpose of financing the salaries and expenses of federal government employees who administer the entitlement program or who perform activities related to these programs. Examples of offices whose salaries and expenses have been financed increasingly by transfers from entitlement programs include: the Agriculture Stabilization and Conservation Service, the Indian Health Service, the Department of Health and Human Service's Office of the Inspector General, and the Office of Personnel Management.

21. Recovery of prior-year obligations reduces budget authority in the same way as collections and transfers from mandatory programs. Unlike the other two, however, recoveries do not reduce outlays; outlays occur from the use of recoveries in the same way they occur from the use of new budget authority; i.e., when payments are made to liquidate the obligations of the funds.

22. U.S. Constitution, Article I, sec. 9, clause 7.

23. U.S. Dept. of Housing and Urban Development, *Budget Justification*, FY 1981, p. C-27. Only budget authority is discussed here because the other forms of budgetary resources are unimportant for the operation of these programs.

24. *Agriculture, Rural Development, and Related Agencies Appropriations Act, 1982*, PL 97-1037. During the mid-1980s the appropriations committees appropriated less than the full amount necessary for interest subsidies and prior-year losses, making supplemental appropriations necessary to provide the amount not included in the basic appropriations act.

25. Although the subsidy value may have declined because of a legislative increase in tenants' rental contributions in 1981, no evidence is available regarding either the size or direction of subsidy changes.

26. The shortening of housing contract length during the 1980s dramatically increased the budget authority requirements for HUD housing programs in the early 1990s. Not only did twenty-year contracts signed in the early 1970s expire, but so also did the five-year contracts signed during the middle of the 1980s. The total number of housing units covered under expiring contracts increased from about 23,500 in fiscal year 1990 to nearly 300,000 in 1991. U.S. Dept. of Housing and Urban Development, *Budget Justification*, FY 1989, p. C-19.

27. For example, in 1988 the annualized cost of a voucher was only about two-thirds of the subsidy cost under various other HUD programs.

28. U.S. OMB, unpublished tables, 1990. A final point about housing programs concerns the relation between budget authority and outlays. Under a long-term contract, budget authority produces very few outlays for the first few years. Thus, the housing outlays in the 1980s resulted mostly from obligations incurred previously. In this sense, the outlays CBO reports for discretionary programs greatly *overstate* the government appropriation for subsidized housing in the year the outlays were recorded.

29. Likewise, budgetary resources, defined as the total amount available for obligation from all sources, gives an equally misleading picture of the size of direct loan activities. Usually, most of the budgetary resources are devoted to liquidating obligations for activities other than issuing loans to the public, such as the payment of interest on prior borrowings from the Treasury and the repayment of outstanding debt to the Treasury.

30. On the need to change accounting techniques for credit, see U.S. OMB, *Proposed Federal Credit Reform Act of 1987*. See also Bosworth, Carron, and Rhyne, *Economics*, and U.S. Congress, CBO, *Credit Reform*. Moreover, there is a growing consensus that in the aggregate, all federal loan programs—discretionary, mandatory, and off-budget through government-sponsored enterprises—are creating an enormous potential liability to federal taxpayers.

31. The commission explained alternative budgetary treatments of credit programs. The debate over the Federal Financing Bank focused principally on the inefficiencies and cost associated with the proliferation of agency debt. Among other reasons, the purpose of the Congressional Budget and Impoundment Control Act was to establish a budget resolu-

tion process by which Congress would consider establishing targets for the total level of spending and revenues prior to beginning action on its individual bills. The debate concerning credit programs considered whether or not these programs would be included in the budget resolution totals and if so, how.

32. The development of the measure of budgetary resources used in this chapter is part of a larger project currently under way to develop a consistent data record of the federal government spending decisions over the post–World War II period.

33. In selecting bureaus, the data for all bureaus were first converted to constant 1989 dollars.

34. Because the overall rise in the general level of prices during the period was 35 percent, a 19 percent constant-dollar increase is equivalent to a 60 percent nominal dollar increase.

35. As measured in budget authority, which constitutes virtually all of the department's new budgetary resources each year, the Reagan administration Defense Department budget growth was 31 percent. This growth measures the increase in the Department of Defense budget over the 1981 budget that had been approved prior to the Reagan administration taking office. That is, the 1981 base amount does not include the action on the 1981 supplemental appropriation that was requested by the Reagan administration.

36. By asserting that additional money spent on revenue agents yielded a greater amount in tax collections, Congress and the Administration could raise the IRS's budget while claiming that the federal budget deficit would be lowered.

37. An exception might be the National Science Foundation, which in 1981 was slated for significant budget reductions. By 1986, however, the President was calling for a doubling of the NSF's budget.

38. Despite the $1.4 billion appropriation cut, the Postal Service's budget increased by 35 percent between 1981 and 1989, after adjusting for inflation. A good portion of this growth was financed by borrowing from the Treasury. During this period, its nominal-dollar debt to the Treasury more than tripled, growing 23 percent faster than the growth in the national debt held by the public during this period.

39. Between 1981, when energy prices reached their historic peak, and 1989, energy prices fell by more than 50 percent relative to the overall level of prices in the economy.

Chapter 5

1. Brady and Morgan, "Reforming the Structure of the House Appropriations Process."

2. The term *backdoor spending* refers to budget authority provided or mandated in authorizing legislation rather than appropriations bills. This type of spending is defined as "spending authority" in the Congressional Budget Act.

3. The annual surplus in the basic Social Security trust funds is projected to double from about $60 billion in fiscal 1991 to $120 billion in fiscal 1996.

4. The tactic of generating incremental revenue that can then be used for incremental expansion of the Social Security program is discussed in Derthick, *Policymaking*.

5. The gross interest paid out of the general fund now exceeds 40 percent of general fund receipts. Arguably this is a more relevant measure of the interest burden than is net interest.

6. These rules changes are identified in Schick, *Congress and Money*, esp. chap. 10, pp. 415–40.

7. Under current law, funds may be deferred only for the limited reasons allowed by the Anti-Deficiency Act; they may not be deferred for policy reasons. In recent years, Congress has failed to approve most of the rescissions proposed by the President.

8. For example, the fiscal 1990 appropriations for the Customs Service (PL 101-136) provides that the service shall have an average "of not less than 16,976 full-time equivalent positions" during the fiscal year.

9. The classic statement on incrementalism as practiced by the appropriations committees and others is Wildavsky's 1964 book, *The Politics of the Budgetary Process*.

10. See Ellwood, *Reductions*.

11. See U.S. Congress, Committee on Budget, HR, *Review of the Reconciliation Process*.

12. In the late 1980s, the appropriations committees were compelled to use baselines because the budget summit agreements set forth the amounts to be saved in appropriations for defense and domestic programs.

13. Meyers, *Strategic Budgeting*.

14. Morgan published at least 38 stories on the appropriations process in 1989–91.

15. Meyers, *Strategic Budgeting*.

Appendix B

1. These concerns were expressed in a series of hearings held by the Joint Economic Committee between 1969 and 1973 regarding setting national priorities. See U.S. Congress, Joint Economic Committee, "Military Budget"; "National Priorities and the Budgetary Process." U.S. Congress, Joint Economic Committee, Subcommittee on Priorities and Economy in

Government, "Changing National Priorities"; "National Priorities and the Budgetary Process"; "National Priorities—the Next Five Years." For academic analysis, see Schick, *Congress and Money*, pp. 52–53, 131–33. On the importance of policy neutrality, see, e.g., Joel Haveman, *Congress and the Budget*, pp. 60–61.

2. U.S. Senate, "Improving Congressional Control of the Budget," pp. 60–61.

3. Ibid., p. 61.

4. U.S. Congress, *Congressional Record, Proceedings and Debates of the 93rd Congress*, First Session, Vol. 119, Part 25, Sept. 28–Oct. 8, 1973.

5. 31 U.S.C. 1109.

6. See *Congressional Record, Proceedings and Debates of the 93rd Congress*, Vol. 120, Part 6, Mar. 19, 1974, p. 7162. See also the similar comments of Senator Byrd, ibid.

7. See, e.g., U.S. Congress, Joint Economic Committee, "1975 Budget"; "1976 Current Services Budget."

8. For definitions similar to those used in this Appendix, see Congressional Quarterly, *Federal Budget Process*; Wildavsky, *New Politics*, p. 442.

9. See, e.g., the Congressional sources in Chap. 3, note 4.

Bibliography

Agriculture, Rural Development, and Related Agencies Appropriations Act, 1982. PL 97-103.

Becker, Gary. *The Economic Approach to Human Behavior.* Chicago: University of Chicago Press, 1976.

Bethel, Tom. "Smoke, Mirrors, and the Adversary Press." *American Spectator* 23 (Dec. 1990): 13–15.

BNA. *Antitrust and Trade Regulation Report* 57. 1989.

Bosworth, Barry P., Andrew S. Carron, and Elisabeth H. Rhyne. *The Economics of Federal Credit Programs.* Washington, D.C.: Brookings Institution, 1987.

Brady, David, and Mark Morgan. "Reforming the Structure of the House Appropriations Process: The Effects of the 1885 and 1919–1920 Reforms on Money Decisions." In *Congress: Structure and Policy*, edited by Matthew D. McCubbins and Terry Sullivan. New York: Cambridge University Press, 1987.

Buchanan, James, and Gordon Tullock. *The Calculus of Consent: Logical Foundations of Constitutional Democracy.* Ann Arbor: University of Michigan Press, 1965.

Code of Federal Regulations, vol. 5, chap. 3, sec. 1310. Washington, D.C., 1991.

Congressional Budget and Impoundment Control Act of 1974. PL 93-344.

Congressional Quarterly. 93rd Cong., 2nd sess. 1974.

———. "The Federal Budget Process: Procedures and Strategies in Congress and the Executive Branch." 1988.

———. "Increase in FHA Mortgage Cap Obtained by Conferees." 1989, p. 2796.

———. "Congress Out to Cut Pay Gap." Aug. 25, 1990, p. 2710.

———. "Parties Wrangle over Power to Figure Cost Overruns." 1990, p. 4072.

Cuny, Thomas J. "Offsetting Collections in the Federal Budget," *Public Budgeting & Finance* 8(3) (1988): 96–110.

Davis, Karen. "Cost Containment and Health Care in the United States." In David Schnall and Carl Figliola, eds., *Contemporary Issues in Health Care*, pp. 37–60. New York: Praeger, 1984.

Demsetz, Harold. "Toward a Theory of Property Rights." *American Economic Review* 57 (2) (May 1967).

Derthick, Martha. *Policymaking for Social Security.* Washington, D.C.: Brookings Institution, 1979.

Dewey, Davis. *The Financial History of the United States.* New York: Longmans, Green, 1931.

Ellwood, John W., ed. *Reductions in U.S. Domestic Spending.* New Brunswick, N.J.: Transaction Books, 1982.

Executive Office of the President, Office of Management and Budget (OMB). *The Budget of the United States Government* (various years).

———. *The Budget of the United States Government Fiscal Year 1977,* Appendix. 1976.

———. *The Budget of the United States Government Fiscal Year 1989, Historical Tables.* 1988.

———. *Special Analysis: Budget of the United States Government, Fiscal Year 1989.* 1988.

Feder, Judith, Jack Hadley, and Steven Zuckerman. "How Did Medicare's Hospital Prospective Payment System Affect Hospitals?" *New England Journal of Medicine* 317, issue 14 (1987): 867–73.

Fenno, Richard. *The Power of the Purse, Appropriations, Politics and Congress.* Boston: Little, Brown, 1966.

Fisher, Louis. *Presidential Spending Power.* Princeton, N.J.: Princeton University Press, 1975.

General Accounting Office (GAO). *Medicare Laboratory Fee Schedules Produced Large Beneficiary Savings but No Program Savings.* Dec. 1987.

———. *Medicare Past Overuse of Intensive Care Services Inflates Hospital Payments.* Mar. 1986.

———. *The President's Current Services Budget.* Jan. 1987.

———. *U.S.D.A.'s Commodity Program: The Accuracy of Budget Forecasts.* Apr. 1988.

Glasson, William. *Federal Military Pensions in the United States.* New York: Oxford University Press, 1918.

Haas, Lawrence. "Budget Focus—Genuine Cut." *National Journal* 19 (1987): 2124.

———. "When a Cut Is Not All That Unkind." *National Journal*, 19 (1987): 2681–82.

Hardin, Garrett. "The Tragedy of the Commons." *Science Magazine* 162 (1968): 1234–48.

Hart, George L. (official reporter). *Sixteenth Republican National Convention.* New York: Tenny Press, 1916.

Haveman, Joel. *Congress and the Budget.* Bloomington: Indiana University Press, 1978.

Heclo, Hugh. "Executive Budget Making." In Gregory B. Mills and John L. Palmer, eds., *Federal Budget Policy in the 1980s*, pp. 255–91. Washington: Urban Institute, 1984.

Hoagland, William. "The Omnibus Budget Reconciliation Act of 1990." Speech before American Enterprise Institute, Japan Economic Foundation, Kyoto, Nov. 19–20, 1990.

Johnston, Bruce. "OMB and the Budget Examiner: Changes in the Reagan Era." *Public Budgeting and Finance* 8(4) (1988): 3–21.

———. "The OMB Examiner and the Congressional Budget Process." *Public Budgeting and Finance* 9(1) (1989): 5–14.

Kamlet, Mark S. "Budgetary Side Payments and Government Growth: 1953–1968." *American Journal of Political Science* 27(4) (1983): 636–64.

Kamlet, Mark S., and David C. Mowery. "The Budgetary Base in Federal Resource Allocation." *American Journal of Political Science* 24 (1980): 804.

———. "Presidential Management of Budgetary and Fiscal Policymaking." *Political Science Quarterly* 95 (Fall 1980): 395–425.

Keith, Robert, and Edward Davis. *Budget Enforcement Act of 1990: Brief Summary.* Washington, D.C.: Congressional Research Services, 1990.

Kremer, Bruce, comp. *Democratic National Convention.* June 1916.

Kusserow, Richard. "Causes of Profits Earned by Hospitals Subject to the Prospective Payment System." Statement before the Subcommittee on Health of the Senate Finance Committee, Apr. 4, 1987.

McCormick, Robert, and Robert Tollison. *Politicians, Legislation, and the Economy: An Inquiry into the Interest-group Theory of Government.* Boston: Nijhoff, Hinghan, 1981.

McNeil, John S., Pedro J. Lecca, and Roosevelt Wright, Jr. *Military Retirement: Social, Economic, and Mental Health Dilemmas.* N.J.: Rowman & Allanheld, 1983.

Meyers, Roy. *Strategic Budgeting.* Ann Arbor: University of Michigan Press, forthcoming.

National Economic Commission. "Democratic Report." Mar. 1, 1989.

———. Staff Papers, Background Papers and Major Testimony. Nov. 30, 1988.

Naylor, E. E. *The Federal Budget System in Operation*. New York: Columbia University Press, 1941.

Olson, James S. *Herbert Hoover and the Reconstruction Finance Corporation, 1931–1933*. Ames: Iowa State University Press, 1977.

Ornstein, Norman J. et al., eds. *Vital Statistics on Congress, 1989–90*. Washington, D.C.: Congress Quarterly Press, 1990.

Patent and Trademark Laws Act, 1980. PL 96-517.

Patent and Trademark Office. Authorizations, Amendments, Schedule of Fees Act, 1982. PL 97-247.

President's Commission on Budget Concepts. *Staff Papers and Other Material Reviewed by the President's Commission*. Washington, D.C.: GPO, 1987.

Presidential Document. *Building a Better America*. Feb. 9, 1989.

Rauch, Jonathan. "The FY 1988 Budget: Round One." *National Journal*, Jan. 10, 1987.

Reagan Administration. "Weekly Compilation of Presidential Documents." Feb. 1981.

———. "Weekly Compilation of Presidential Documents." Mar. 1981.

Schick, Allen. *The Capacity to Budget*. Washington, D.C.: Urban Institute, 1990.

———. *Congress and Money: Budgeting, Spending and Taxing*. Washington, D.C.: Urban Institute, 1980.

———. "How the Budget Was Won and Lost." In Norman J. Ornstein, ed., *President and Congress: Assessing Reagan's First Year*. Washington, D.C.: American Enterprise Institute, 1982.

———. *Legislation, Appropriations, and Budgets: The Development of Spending Decision-Making in Congress*, Report 84-106. Washington, D.C.: Congressional Research Service, May 1984.

Schwartz, Gary. "Urban Freeways and the Interstate System." *Southern California Law Review* 49 (1976): 406–513.

Stewart, Charles. "Changes in Latitude, Changes in Magnitude. Spending Decisions and Institution in the House after the Civil War." Paper presented at the Hoover Institution, conference on Legislative Institutions, Practices and Behavior, Feb. 26–27, 1988.

U.S. Congress. Committee on the Budget, House of Representatives. *Congressional Control and Expenditures*. Jan. 1977.

———. ———. *A Review of the Reconciliation Process*. Committee Print, Oct. 1984.

———. Committee on the Budget, Senate. *The President's 1989 Budget: Overview and Analysis*, Feb. 1988.

———. ———. *Framework for the 1990 Budget Resolution: Implementing the Bipartisan Budget Resolution*. 1989.

———. Congressional Budget Office (CBO). *The Budgetary Treatment of Federal Civilian Agency Pay Raises: A Technical Analysis*. Jan. 1983.
———. ———. *Credit Reform: Comparable Budget Costs for Cash and Credit*. 1989.
———. ———. *The Economic and Budget Outlook: Fiscal Years 1986–1990*. Feb. 1985.
———. ———. *The Economic and Budget Outlook: Fiscal Years 1989–1993*. 1988.
———. ———. *The Economic and Budget Outlook: Fiscal Years 1991–1995*. Jan. 1990.
———. ———. *The Economic and Budget Outlook: Fiscal Years 1990–1995*. Feb. 1990.
———. ———. *The Economic and Budget Outlook: Fiscal Years 1992–1996*. Feb. 1991.
———. ———. *Including Capital Expenses in the Prospective Payment System*. Aug. 1988.
———. ———. *The NASA Program in the 1990's and Beyond*. May 1988.
———. ———. *Operations and Support Costs for the Department of Defense*. July 1988.
———. ——— (staff memorandum). *Pay-As-You-Go Budgeting*. Mar. 1990.
———. ———. *Physician Reimbursement Under Medicare: Options for Change*. April 1986.
———. ———. *A Profile of the Congressional Budget Office*. Sept. 1990.
———. *Congressional Globe*. Washington, D.C.: GPO, Mar. 2, 1865.
———. *Congressional Record, Proceedings and Debates of the Congress*, various issues. Washington, D.C.: GPO.
———. House of Representatives (HR), Committee on Appropriations. *Hearings Before the Subcommittee on Rural Development, Agriculture, and Related Agencies Appropriations for 1988*.
———. House of Representatives, Committee on Ways and Means. *Background Material and Data on Programs Within the Jurisdiction of the Committee on Ways and Means*. Washington, D.C.: GPO, 1984, 1987, 1990.
———. Joint Economic Committee (staff study). "The 1975 Budget: An Advance Look." Dec. 23, 1973.
———. ——— (staff study). "The 1976 Current Services Budget." Dec. 31, 1974.
———. ———. "The Military Budget and National Economic Priorities Hearings Before the Subcommittee on Economy in Government." June 1969.

———. Joint Economic Committee, Subcommittee on Priorities and Economy in Government. "Changing National Priorities—The Next Five Years." Hearings, May and June 1972.

———. ———. "The Military Budget and National Economic Priorities Hearings Before the Subcommittee on Economy in Government." Hearings, June 1969.

———. ———. "National Priorities and the Budgetary Process." Hearings, 93rd Cong., 1st sess., Apr. 25, 26, 27, 1973.

———. ———. "National Priorities—the Next Five Years." Hearings, 92nd Cong., 2nd sess., May 30–June 27, 1972.

———. Report on the activities of the Senate Finance Committee. 98th Cong., 1st sess. Washington, D.C.: GPO, 1984.

———. Report of the Senate Committee on Banking, Housing and Urban Affairs (summary of activities). 98th Cong., 2nd sess. Washington, D.C.: GPO, Dec. 1984.

———. Reports on the activities of various House committees (nos. 994, 1018, 1025–26, 1043–45). 99th Cong., 2nd sess. Washington, D.C.: GPO, 1987.

———. Reports on the activities of various Senate committees (nos. 6, 9, 10, 12, 17–19, 21, 25, 32, 35). 99th Cong., 1st sess. Washington, D.C.: GPO, Jan. 1987.

U.S. Department of Commerce, Bureau of the Census. *Statistical Abstract of the United States, 1979*. Washington, D.C.

———. *Statistical Abstract of the United States, 1988*. Washington, D.C.

U.S. Department of Health and Human Services. *Justification of Budget and Legislative Program for Fiscal Year 1983*.

U.S. Department of Housing and Urban Development. *Budget Justification* (various years). Washington, D.C.

U.S. Department of Labor. *Budget Justifications of Appropriation Estimates for Committee on Appropriations*. Jan. 1984, Feb. 1986.

U.S. Department of the Treasury. *Annual Report of the Secretary of the Treasury on the State of Finances*. Washington, D.C.: GPO, 1941–51.

———. *Annual Report of the Secretary of the Treasury on the State of Finances*, statistical appendix. Washington, D.C.: GPO, 1980.

———. *Digest of Appropriations*. Washington, D.C.: GPO, 1939.

U.S. Office of Management and Budget (OMB). *Budget of the United States Government*. Washington, D.C.: GPO, annual issues 1934, 1947, 1952–91.

———. *Budget of the United States Government: Fiscal Year 1992, Historical Tables*. Washington, D.C.: GPO, 1991.

———. *Proposed Federal Credit Reform Act of 1987*. Washington, D.C., GPO, Mar. 1987.

———. *Special Analyses of the United States Budget.* Washington, D.C.: GPO, 1952–91.

———. Unpublished tables. 1990.

U.S. Senate, Budget Committee Majority. "Updated Summary of the Conference Budget Reconciliation Bill," Oct. 30, 1990.

U.S. Senate, Committee on the Budget. Omnibus Budget Reconciliation Act of 1987. Conference Report to Accompany H.R. 3545. Dec. 21, 1987.

U.S. Senate, Committee on the Budget (Staff). *The President's 1989 Budget: Overview and Analysis.* Feb. 18, 1988.

———. *Framework for the 1990 Budget Resolution: Implementing the Bipartisan Budget Agreement*, Apr. 18, 1989.

———. "Improving Congressional Control of the Budget." Hearings before the Subcommittee on Budgeting, Management, and Expenditures of the Committee on Government Operations, May 7, 1973.

U.S. Statutes at Large. 37th Cong., 2nd sess., ch. 166. Washington, D.C.: GPO, 1862.

———. 74th Cong., 1st sess., ch. 531. Washington, D.C.: GPO, 1935.

Wildavsky, Aaron. *The New Politics of the Budgetary Process.* Glenview, Ill.: Scott, Foresman, 1988.

———. *The Politics of the Budgetary Process.* Boston: Little, Brown, 1964.

Willoughby, W. F. *The National Budget System.* Baltimore: Johns Hopkins University Press, 1927.

Index

In this index an "f" after a number indicates a separate reference on the next page, and an "ff" indicates separate references on the next two pages. A continuous discussion over two or more pages is indicated by a span of page numbers, e.g., "57–59." *Passim* is used for a cluster of references in close but not consecutive sequence.

Library of Congress Cataloguing-in-Publication Data

Cogan, John F.
The budget puzzle : understanding federal spending / John F. Cogan, Timothy J. Muris, and Allen Schick
p. cm.
Includes bibliographical references and index.
ISBN 0-8047-2091-6 (cloth: acid-free paper). —
ISBN 0-8047-2092-4 (paper: acid-free paper)
1. Budget—United States. 2. Government spending policy—United States. I. Muris, Timothy J. II. Schick, Allen. III. Title.
HJ2051.C556 1994
336.3'9'0973—dc 20 93-31627
CIP

⊗ This book is printed on acid-free paper.